JOHN BUNYAN ON PRAYER

31 PRAYER INSIGHTS FROM THE AUTHOR OF
"THE PILGRIM'S PROGRESS."

GODLIPRESS TEAM

© Copyright 2022 by GodliPress. All rights reserved.

This book is copyright protected. You cannot amend, distribute, sell, use, quote or paraphrase any part, or the content within this book, without the consent of the author or publisher, except in the case of brief quotations embodied in critical articles or reviews.

Unless otherwise indicated, all Scripture quotations are from The ESV® Bible (The Holy Bible, English Standard Version®), copyright © 2001 by Crossway, a publishing ministry of Good News Publishers. Used by permission. All rights reserved.

CONTENTS

Introduction	vii
1. WHAT IS PRAYER?	1
Daily Reflection	4
2. WHAT IS PRAYER? (CONTINUED)	5
Daily Reflection	7
3. ENCOURAGEMENTS IN PRAYER	9
Daily Reflection	12
4. PRAYING IN THE SPIRIT	13
Daily Reflection	15
5. PRAYING IN THE SPIRIT WITH UNDERSTANDING	17
Daily Reflection	20
6. OBSTRUCTIONS TO PRAYER	21
Daily Reflection	24
7. UNITY BRINGS PRAYER	25
Daily Reflection	27
8. GOD'S WAYS OF ANSWERING	29
Daily Reflection	32
9. THE FEAR OF GOD BRINGS US TO PRAY	34
Daily Reflection	36
10. BENEFITS OF PRAYER	38
Daily Reflection	40
11. DEALING WITH DISCOURAGEMENTS IN PRAYER	42
Daily Reflection	44

12. THE PHARISEE'S PRAYER	46
Daily Reflection	49
13. THE TAX COLLECTOR'S PRAYER	50
Daily Reflection	52
14. THE POWER OF THE TONGUE	53
Daily Reflection	55
15. UNANSWERED PRAYERS	57
Daily Reflection	60
16. PRAYING WITHOUT THE SPIRIT	61
Daily Reflection	63
17. A PRAYER TOO LATE	65
Daily Reflection	67
18. CENSERS OF PRAYER	69
Daily Reflection	71
19. ALTAR OF INCENSE	73
Daily Reflection	75
20. PRAY FOR YOUR MIND AND WILL	77
Daily Reflection	79
21. COMMITTING YOUR SOUL TO GOD	81
Daily Reflection	83
22. CLOSET SIN	85
Daily Reflection	88
23. PRAYER OF A BROKEN HEART	89
Daily Reflection	92
24. A HIGH PRIEST WHO INTERCEDES	93
Daily Reflection	95
25. CRYING OUT TO GOD	97
Daily Reflection	100
26. PERSEVERING IN PRAYER	101
Daily Reflection	103

27. JESUS PRAYS FOR US	105
Daily Reflection	107
28. JESUS PRAYS FOR US (CONTINUED)	109
Daily Reflection	111
29. THOSE WHO DO NOT PRAY	113
Daily Reflection	115
30. THE THRONE OF GRACE	117
Daily Reflection	119
31. COMING BOLDLY TO THE THRONE	121
Daily Reflection	123
About John Bunyan	125
Bibliography	129

INTRODUCTION

John Bunyan lived over 200 years ago, and yet he is still a household name today because of his classic allegorical story about a man named Christian who travels to the Celestial City and meets a host of characters along the way. Most of us are aware that he wrote this famous story called *The Pilgrim's Progress*. It has been translated, adapted into different versions, and made into movies; an allegory of our journey through the Christian life. Most bookshelves in homes, shops, and churches proudly house a copy, making it a firm classic around the world.

But hardly anyone is aware of any of his other works, even though he wrote almost 60 books, leaflets, and allegorical stories!

His unapologetic and simple approach is evident in his writing, where he was not afraid to say it like it is and draw a line between black and white. This style made him popular with many people in his day, and equally unpopular with those whose feet he trod upon as he proclaimed a Puritan Gospel.

Having spent many years in the Bedford jail over 200 years ago, he had enough time on his hands to write, and we are blessed to still have access to such rich insight into many topics, ranging from the temple and its many facets down to our simple daily walk with the Lord. In all of this, he acknowledges prayer as a key aspect of Christian living.

Drawing from this wealth of knowledge and inspiration for this compilation on prayer has been rewarding in bringing his work to a modern audience. Keeping true to the heart of his message, we have updated phrases and words but kept the meaning as clear as it was back then. Some parts and passages have been abridged, while others have been joined together to bring the best parts into one book concentrated on a single topic.

The 31-day format makes it more accessible and easy to read and apply these nuggets of spiritual information into our busy lives. Setting apart a month to work through the book gives one enough time to absorb the rich jewels that shine out in Bunyan's work. As an added feature, daily reflections will allow you to search and self-reflect on the different topics. Use these, as you will gain more out of each chapter. They are not there to be strictly adhered to but rather to be used as signposts that can lead you into deeper thought on each topic.

John Bunyan's goal was that people would wake up and see the beauty, necessity, and urgency of prayer. By bringing you this book in this format, we hope that he will reach this goal with you as the reader. Allow your eyes to be opened, your heart to be challenged, and your prayer to rise to the throne of grace.

"In prayer, it is better to have a heart without words than words without a heart. "

1
WHAT IS PRAYER?

"Then you will call upon me and come and pray to me, and I will hear you"
—Jeremiah 29:12

What is prayer? Prayer is a sincere, aware, passionate pouring out of the heart or soul to God through Jesus, in the strength and assistance of the Holy Spirit, for things that God has promised, or according to the Word, for the good of the church, with submission, in faith, to the will of God.

1. It is a **sincere** pouring out of the soul to God. David speaks of sincerity when he mentions prayer: *"I cried to him,"* the Lord *"with my mouth, and high praise was on my tongue. If I had cherished iniquity in my heart, the Lord*

would not have listened" to my prayer (Psalm 66:17-18). Without sincerity, God does not see it as real prayer (Psalm 16:1-4). *"Then you will call upon me and come and pray to me, and I will hear you. You will seek me and find me, when you seek me with all your heart"* (Jer. 29:12-13). Because of this, God rejected their prayers in Hosea 7:14, where he says, *"They do not cry to me from the heart."*

Jesus commended the sincerity in Nathaniel when he was under the fig tree. *"Behold, an Israelite indeed, in whom there is no deceit"* (John 1:47). The prayer that has this in it as one of the main ingredients is the prayer that God looks at. Then, *"the prayer of the upright is acceptable to him"* (Prov. 15:8). Sincerity brings the soul to open its heart to God, and to tell Him everything plainly, without ambiguity; to condemn itself plainly, without pretending; to cry to God passionately, without flattery.

Sincerity is the same in a quiet corner as it is before the world. It is not lip-service, because it is the heart that God looks at, and from sincerity that prayer comes from if it is sincere prayer.

1. It is a sincere and **aware** pouring out of the heart or soul. It is not a few complimentary expressions, but awareness in the heart. Prayer is aware of sin and mercy received.

Real prayer bubbles out of the heart when overcome with grief (1 Sam. 1:10). David roars, cries, and weeps (Psalm

38:8-10). Hezekiah mourns like a dove (Isa. 38:14). Ephraim bemoans himself (Jer. 31:18). Peter weeps bitterly (Matt. 26:75). Jesus cries strong tears (Heb. 5:7). All this comes from a sense of the justice of God, the guilt of sin, and the pains of hell and destruction.

Sometimes there is a sweet sense of mercy received. David pours out his soul to bless God for his lovingkindness in Psalm 103:1-5.

1. Prayer is a sincere, aware, and **passionate** pouring out of the soul to God.

- *"As a deer pants for flowing streams, so pants my soul for you, O God"* (Psalm 42:1).
- *"My soul longs, yes, faints for the courts of the Lord; my heart and flesh sing for joy to the living God"* (Psalm 84:2).
- *"My soul is consumed with longing for your rules at all times."* (Psalm 119:20).

This is called the fervent, or the working prayer, by James. And so again, *"And being in agony he prayed more earnestly"* (Luke 22:44). When passion is engaged in prayer, then the whole person is engaged, it is a pouring out of the heart or soul. *"O Lord, all my longing is before you;"* says David, *"my sighing is not hidden from you"* (Psalm 38:9).

1. It is a sincere, aware, passionate pouring out of the heart or soul to God, **through Jesus**. Without Jesus, we must ask whether it is prayer, even though it sounds eloquent. Jesus is the way through whom we

are admitted to God. *"Whatever you ask in my name"; "If you ask me anything in my name, I will do it"* (John 14:13-14). This was Daniel's way of praying for the people of God; he did it in the name of Jesus. *"Now therefore, O our God, listen to the prayer of your servant and to his pleas for mercy, and for your own sake, O Lord, make your face to shine upon your sanctuary"* (Dan. 9:17). And so David, *"For your name's sake,"* that is, for thy Christ's sake, *"pardon my guilt, for it is great"* (Psalm 25:11).

Whoever is born again becomes one of the sons of God, and is joined to Jesus (John 3:5,7; 1:12). As a part of Christ, part of his body, the Spirit is shown in that person's heart by God (Eph. 5:30). In Jesus' blood, righteousness, victory, and intercession, they stand before Him; *"He has blessed us in the Beloved"* (Eph. 1:6).

Daily Reflection

Everybody has some idea of what prayer is. Bunyan makes it very clear in this chapter by outlining a statement about it, and then breaking that down piece by piece. This can be helpful with doing a self-assessment of the different aspects and whether they are evident in your own prayer life or not.

1. How would you rate your prayer life?
2. Are you aware of pouring out your heart during your prayers?
3. Do you pray passionately and fervently?
4. Do you assume you are praying in and through Jesus, or are you conscious of it every time?

2

WHAT IS PRAYER? (CONTINUED)

*"You will seek me and find me, when you seek me
with all your heart"*
—Jeremiah 29:13

What is prayer? Prayer is a sincere, aware, passionate pouring out of the heart or soul to God through Jesus, in the strength and assistance of the Holy Spirit, for things that God has promised, or according to the Word, for the good of the church, with submission, in faith, to the will of God.

1. Prayer is a sincere, aware, passionate pouring out of the heart or soul to God through Jesus, by the strength or **assistance of the Spirit**. If it's not in the strength and assistance of the Spirit, it is like the

sons of Aaron, offering strange fire on the altar (Lev. 10:1-2).

2. Prayer is a sincere, aware, passionate pouring out of the heart, or soul, to God, through Jesus, in the strength and assistance of the Spirit, **for things that God has promised**. Prayer is true when it is in line with God's Word; it is blasphemy, or useless words, when it is not. So, David in prayer kept his eye on the Word of God. *"My soul,"* he said, *"clings to the dust; give me life according to your word!"* And again, *"My soul melts away for sorrow; strengthen me according to your word!"* And, *"Remember your word to your servant, in which you have made me hope"* (Psalm 119:25, 28, 49).

The Spirit by the Word must direct us in prayer. *"I will pray with my spirit, but I will pray with my mind also"* (1 Cor. 14:15). There is no understanding without the Word. For if they reject the word of the Lord, *"what wisdom is in them?"* (Jer. 8:9).

1. **For the good of the church**. This relates to God's glory, the spread of the Gospel, or the benefit of God's people. We must pray for grace for the church, for help against temptations; that God would let nothing be too hard for it; and that all things might work together for its good, that God would keep the church blameless and harmless, the sons of God, to His glory, in the midst of a crooked and perverse nation. This is the substance of Jesus' own prayer in John 17. And all Paul's prayers are the same, as Philippians 1:9-11 shows: *"And it is my prayer that your*

love may abound more and more, with knowledge and all discernment, so that you may approve what is excellent, and so be pure and blameless for the day of Christ, filled with the fruit of righteousness that comes through Jesus Christ, to the glory and praise of God."

2. Prayer must **submit to the will of God**, and say, *"Your will be done, on earth as it is in heaven"* (Matt. 6:10); therefore, we must lay ourselves and our prayers, and all that we have, at the feet of God, to be used by him as He sees best. When we pray with submission to the will of God, we do not doubt or question God's love and kindness to us. *"And this is the confidence that we have toward him, that if we ask anything according to his will he hears us. And if we know that he hears us in whatever we ask, we know that we have the requests that we have asked of him,"* that is, we ask in the Spirit of grace and supplication (1 John 5:14-15).

The prayer that is not through the Spirit will not be answered, because it is beside the will of God. The Spirit only knows the will of God. *"For who knows a person's thoughts except the spirit of that person, which is in him? So also no one comprehends the thoughts of God except the Spirit of God"* (1 Cor. 2:11).

Daily Reflection

Continuing with Bunyan's concise, descriptive definition of prayer, we can further assess how our own prayers match up. It is not a condemnation if they fall short of his statement, but rather an opportunity to see where we need to work or change in order to realize a much better, fuller prayer life.

1. Are you aware of the Spirit's help during prayer? Do you ask for it?
2. Do you ever acknowledge and build your prayers around God's promises as a foundation?
3. How is praying good for the church as a whole? Do you ever include your church, fellow Christians, and pastor in your prayers?
4. Are your prayers in line with God's will? How do you know if they are?
5. Having gone through these two chapters, how do your prayers match up?

3

ENCOURAGEMENTS IN PRAYER

"There I will meet with you, and from above the mercy seat… I will speak with you about all that I will give you"
—Exodus 25:22

These are encouragements for the poor, tempted, and depressed to pray to God through Christ.

1. Luke 11 is very encouraging for anyone who hungers after Jesus. In verses 5-7, there is a parable of a man who went to borrow bread and was denied because his friend was in bed. But because of his perseverance, the friend got up and gave it to him, clearly showing that even though we cannot see that we are the friends of God, yet we should never stop

asking, seeking, and knocking at God's door for mercy.

Jesus says, *"I tell you, though he will not get up and give him anything because he is his friend, yet because of his impudence he will rise and give him whatever he needs"* (Luke 11:8). Perhaps you feel like an enemy in your heart because of your wicked works (Col. 1:21), and you think the Lord will tell you not to trouble Him, but continue knocking, crying, and moaning. He will *"rise and give him whatever he needs."*

We find the same thing in Luke 18, in the parable of the unjust judge and the poor widow; her persistence succeeded with him. There is nothing that succeeds with God like persistence. Is it not the same with beggars that come to your door? Though you do not want to give them anything, yet if they follow you, crying out, you will give to them.

1. Another encouragement is to consider the place, throne, or seat on which God sits to hear the petitions and prayers—a *"throne of grace"* (Heb. 4:16); *"The mercy seat"* (Exodus 25:22). God has sat down in mercy and forgiveness; and from there, hears the sinner and speaks with him.

We often think strange thoughts about God and how he handles us, concluding that He will have nothing to do with us, when in fact, He is on the mercy seat and will hear and listen to our prayers. You might be afraid and turn from the face of His Majesty, but when He says, *"There I will meet with you… I will speak with you,"* this should encourage us and give us hope to *"draw near to the throne of grace, that we may receive mercy and find grace to help in time of need"* (Heb. 4:16).

1. Another encouragement to continue in prayer with God is that the mercy seat is continually sprinkled with Jesus' blood. It is called *"sprinkled blood"* (Heb. 12:24). When the high priest under the law went into the holiest, where the mercy seat was, he did not go in *"without taking blood"* (Heb. 9:7). This was because, though God was on the mercy seat, he was perfectly just as well as merciful. The blood was to stop justice from coming down on those in the intercession of the high priest, as in Leviticus 16:13-17, to show that all your unworthiness should not stop you from coming to God in Christ for mercy.

The value of the blood of Jesus sprinkled on the mercy seat stops the course of justice, and opens a floodgate for the mercy of the Lord to be extended to you. Then you have, *"confidence to enter the holy places by the blood of Jesus,"* which has made a *"new and living way"* for you (Heb. 10:19-20). Jesus is there, not only to sprinkle the mercy seat with his blood, but He speaks, and His blood speaks; so that God *"will pass over you, and no plague will befall you to destroy you"* (Exodus 12:13).

Be sober and humble; go to the Father in the name of the Son, and tell Him your case, with the Spirit's help, and you will feel the benefit of praying with the Spirit and with understanding.

Daily Reflection

Dealing with unanswered prayer, times of silence, and our own condemnation and feelings, we can sometimes lose sight of reaching Jesus in our prayers. When we feel low and discouraged in our prayers, it is always good to receive some motivation and inspiration to help us carry on. Bunyan gives us three clear encouragements here. Take your time to absorb them and see how they can move you back into a place of speaking and listening to God.

1. What do you understand by the parables of the persistent friend and the widow?
2. How does this pertain to us? Are you able to apply this to your own prayer life?
3. Why is the picture of Jesus sitting, waiting for us to speak, such an encouragement?
4. How does the blood of Jesus impact prayer?

4

PRAYING IN THE SPIRIT

*"For we do not know what to pray for as we ought,
but the Spirit himself intercedes for us with groanings too deep for
words. And he who searches hearts knows what is the mind of the
Spirit, because the Spirit intercedes for the saints according
to the will of God"*
—Romans 8:26-27

Here, Paul is speaking on behalf of all the apostles: *"For we."* We apostles, the wise master-builders, *"we do not know what to pray for."* We do not know what things we should pray for, to whom we pray, or through whom we pray; none of these things we know, but by the help and assistance of the Spirit. Should we pray for communion with God through Christ? Should we pray for faith, justification by grace, and a sanctified heart? None of these things we know.

"For who knows a person's thoughts except the spirit of that person, which is in him? So also no one comprehends the thoughts of God except the Spirit of God" (1 Cor. 2:11). He speaks of inner and spiritual things that the world does not know about (Isa. 29:11).

He adds, *"we do not know what to pray for as we ought"*; but the Spirit helps our weaknesses, with sighs and groans which are not words. They could not even perform this duty of praying, as we sometimes think we can. Paul says we must pray *"as we ought,"* and this we cannot do by our own abilities, *"but the Spirit himself."* Only the Spirit. Not the Spirit and our ways or what our brain can imagine and devise. While we pray, God is searching the heart, to see what root and spirit it comes from (1 John 5:14). *"And he who searches hearts knows"*; he sees and approves, *"because the Spirit intercedes for the saints according to the will of God."* When it is according to His will, he hears us and nothing else. And it is only the Spirit that can teach us to ask in this way; because only He is able to search out all things, even the deep things of God.

Without the Spirit, even though we have a thousand prayer books, we would not know what we should pray for as we ought, because our weaknesses make us absolutely incapable of doing so. What are these weaknesses? Without the Spirit, we cannot think one right thought about God, which is why God is not in all our thoughts (Psalm 10:4) and *"every intention of the thoughts of his heart was only evil continually"* (Gen. 6:5). How will we be able to address ourselves to God then, without the Spirit's help?

True prayer must come from what the heart sees in the light of the Spirit, because the heart and tongue do not agree unless the Spirit helps our weaknesses. David could not speak one true word, except when the Spirit gave him words.

The Pharisees' prayers were rejected. They were able to express themselves very well for a long time so that everyone noticed, but they did not have the Spirit of Jesus to help them. Therefore, it was only done in their weaknesses, and they fell short of properly pouring out of their souls to God through the strength of the Spirit.

It must be in or with the Spirit because without that, no one can know how to come to God the right way. We can easily say we come to God in His Son, but it is the hardest thing to come to God without the Spirit. It is *"the Spirit"* that *"searches everything, even the depths of God"* (1 Cor. 2:10).

Daily Reflection

Bunyan is very clear that without the Spirit, our prayers fall very short. He gives our weak prayers the strength and capacity to reach heaven. It is one of His main duties—to help us in our prayers. Even as you work through these questions, ask Him to open your eyes, to show you things, and to help you to understand, as it is only through the Spirit that we can truly have a revelation of prayer.

1. Does it surprise you that Paul admits he and the other apostles did not know what they should pray for?

2. What do you understand by, "Not the Spirit and our ways or what our brain can imagine and devise"?
3. What does it mean that the Spirit "intercedes for us"?
4. Why do you think our minds and the Spirit are often in contrast to each other?
5. What is the meaning of 1 Corinthians 2:10?

5

PRAYING IN THE SPIRIT WITH UNDERSTANDING

"I will pray with my spirit, but I will pray with my mind also; I will sing praise with my spirit, but I will sing with my mind also"
—1 Corinthians 14:15

What is it to pray with the Spirit, and to also pray with understanding? Paul puts a clear distinction between the two when he says, *"will pray with my spirit, but I will pray with my mind also."* This was because the Corinthians were using the gifts to puff themselves up instead of to edify the body. So he said, *"if I pray in a tongue, my spirit prays but my mind is unfruitful"* (1 Cor. 14:14).

Understanding must be in prayer, as well as in the heart and mouth. That which is done with understanding is more effective, sensitive, and passionate than that which is done without it. That is why Paul prayed for the Colossians, that God would fill them *"with the knowledge of His will in all spiritual wisdom and understanding"* (Col. 1:9). And for the Ephesians, that God would give them *"the Spirit of wisdom and of revelation in the knowledge of him"* (Eph. 1:17). And for the Philippians, that God would make them abound *"with knowledge and all discernment"* (Phil. 1:9).

To pray with understanding is to pray as the Spirit instructs in the understanding of what is needed to pray for. The church of the Laodiceans wanted knowledge or spiritual understanding, but they did not know that they were poor, wretched, blind, and naked. This made everything they did so insulting to Jesus that He threatened to spew them out of His mouth (Rev. 3:16-17). People without understanding may say the same words in prayer as others do, but if one has understanding and the other has none, there is a huge difference in speaking the same words!

Spiritual understanding sees a readiness and willingness in the heart of God to give those things that the soul needs. David could guess the thoughts of God toward him (Psalm 40:5). It was the same with the woman of Canaan, who by faith and understanding discerned a tenderness and willingness in Jesus' heart to save, despite his words. This made her persistent until she received the mercy she needed (Matt. 15:22-28). Understanding the willingness that is in the heart of God to save sinners will cause you to force the soul to seek more after God, and to cry for pardon.

If someone sees a pearl in a ditch worth a hundred pounds but did not know its value, he would pass by. But if he found out how much it was worth, he would do everything for it. So it is with souls concerning the things of God. If someone understands the worth of them, then his heart runs after them, and he will not stop calling out until he has them. The two blind men in the gospel, because they knew that Jesus was both able and willing to heal their eyes, cried out. The more they were rebuked, the more they cried (Matt. 20:29-31).

The enlightened understanding sees great promises that encourage it to pray and strengthens it. When people promise things, it is encouraging to know what promises are made and to come and ask for them. The understanding also sees arguments that can be used as Jacob did (Gen. 32:9). When Ephraim understood his state before the Lord, he began to lament (Jer. 31:18-20). And in this, he used such arguments with the Lord that it affected his heart, drew out forgiveness, and made Ephraim pleasant in his eyes through Jesus. In response, God said, *"I have heard Ephraim grieving, 'You have disciplined me, and I was disciplined, like an untrained calf; bring me back that I may be restored, for you are the Lord my God. For after I had turned away, I relented, and after I was instructed, I struck my thigh; I was ashamed, and I was confounded, because I bore the disgrace of my youth.'"*

So, you see that we must pray with the Spirit as well as with the understanding.

In my own experience, I have sometimes been in agony in my spirit and felt so strongly to stop seeking the Lord. But understanding what great sinners the Lord has had mercy on, and how large His promises are to sinners; and that it was not the whole, but the sick, not the righteous, but the sinner, not the full, but the empty, that He extends his grace and mercy to. This made me, through the assistance of his Holy Spirit, draw closer to Him, hang on to Him, and cry, even though He did not answer right away. May the Lord help all who are poor, tempted, and in trials to do the same, and to continue, even though it is long, as the prophet spoke about it (Hab. 2:3). May He help them to pray, not by the inventions of men, and their structured formats, but *"will pray with my spirit, but I will pray with my mind also."*

Daily Reflection

After reading the previous chapter, where our minds are often in conflict with what the Spirit wants and does, this chapter can be confusing. But Paul is clear in being practical. It is not what we understand in our own thinking, but to understand what the Spirit is showing us. To be spiritually minded and know God's will—this is the key to effective prayer.

1. Do you find it easy to pray in the Spirit?
2. What do spiritual wisdom and understanding mean to you?
3. What is the meaning of the pearl in the ditch when it comes to praying in the Spirit and with understanding?
4. What are the different things that spiritual understanding brings to prayer?
5. How did the Spirit bring understanding to Bunyan?

6

OBSTRUCTIONS TO PRAYER

*"If I had cherished iniquity in my heart,
the Lord would not have listened"*
—Psalm 66:18

As prayer is the duty of every child of God, by the Spirit of Christ in the heart, so everyone who prays needs to be careful to do it with reverence as well as the mercy of God through Jesus. Prayer draws a person near to God, and therefore, calls for more of God's grace and assistance to help pray when in His presence. It is embarrassing for someone to behave irreverently before a king, but a sin to do it before God. And as a king is not pleased with a speech of inappropriate words and gestures, so God takes no pleasure in the sacrifice of fools (Eccl. 5:1, 4).

It is not long speeches or eloquent tongues that please the ears of the Lord but a humble, broken, and contrite heart, that is sweet in His nostrils (Psalm 51:17; Isa. 57:15). Therefore, there are three things that are obstructions to prayer, and even cancel any requests we might make.

1. When we have sin in our hearts while praying before God. *"If I had cherished iniquity in my heart, the Lord would not have listened"* to my prayer (Psalm 66:18). For this is the wickedness of our hearts, that we will love and hold onto the thing we pray against.

This is a person who honors God with their mouth, but their heart is far from Him (Isa. 29:13; Eze. 33:31). It's like seeing a beggar ask for food and then throwing it to the dogs! It's like saying with one breath for something, and with the next, refusing it! It is saying, "Thy will be done," but not meaning it in our hearts. With our mouths we say, "Hallowed be thy name," and with our hearts and lives, we dishonor him all day long.

These are prayers that become sin (Psalm 109:7), and though we say them often, the Lord will never answer them (2 Sam. 22:42).

1. When men pray to be heard and seen as good Christians. These prayers fall short of God's approval and are never answered. There are two sorts of people who pray like this:
2. Your pretend pastors pretending to worship God when they are really only concerned about their own

welfare and profit. Ahab's prophets and Nebuchadnezzar's wise men pretended to have great devotion, yet their lusts and their bellies were the aims in everything they did.
3. Those who look for recognition and applause for their wonderful words and want to tickle the ears of those listening more than anything else. They pray to be heard and have already received their reward (Matt. 6:5). You can recognize these people by the following:
4. They are only worried about how they sound.
5. They look for commendation when they have finished.
6. Their hearts rest on whether they receive praise or not.
7. The length of their prayer pleases them and they will even repeat things over and over (Matt. 6:7).

These people study to become better but are not worried about the heart behind it all. They look for returns, but it is the useless applause of men. They do not like to be in a prayer room alone but among people. Even if their conscience urges them to go pray alone, hypocrisy will push them to be heard in the streets. When they are done speaking, their prayers end because they do not wait to hear what the Lord will say (Psalm 85:8).

1. A third prayer that will not be accepted by God is when we pray for the wrong things, or if we pray for the right things, but our intention is to use them for our own lusts and for the wrong reasons. Some do

not have because they ask not, James says, and others ask and do not have because they ask incorrectly, that they may consume it on their lusts (James 4:2-4). If the result is contrary to God's will, it will go against the requests presented before Him. So, many people pray for this and that and yet do not receive it. God only answers them with silence. They just have their words for their effort and nothing else.

Daily Reflection

Often we find that our prayers are blocked, or they seem to hit the ceiling and go no further. Aside from God actually hearing us and choosing to wait before answering, there are things in our lives that can cause our prayers to fall flat and never reach God. Bunyan, in his straightforward approach, lists these for our benefit. If they are in your life, it is to help you see so that you can deal with the issue and free the access route of prayer to God again.

1. What does it mean to come to God with reverence in prayer?
2. Why does sin in our hearts block prayer?
3. Why do you think people pray to be heard and seen rather than actually praying to God?
4. Read Matthew 6:5. What does it mean that they have already received their reward?
5. How does this contrast with Matthew 6:6?

7
UNITY BRINGS PRAYER

"For where two or three are gathered in my name, there am I among them"
—Matthew 18:20

Look at those churches where there is peace and you will find growth and prosperity. When churches are at peace and have rest, they are not only multiplied, but, as they walk in the fear of the Lord and the guidance of the Holy Spirit, they are built up. It is when the whole body is knit together, like joints, that churches increase with the increase of God.

This unity and peace come from our joining and agreeing to pray for, and seek, the truths of God that we do not know. The disciples were aware of their imperfections, and so, in one accord, they continued in prayer and supplications. If we were more aware of our own failings and imperfections, we would carry them better with those that are different from us. We would grow more in humility and patience, that we might bring others, or be brought by others, to the knowledge of the truth. If we all agreed that we were failing in many things, we would soon agree to go to God and pray for more wisdom and revelation of His mind and will concerning us.

Where unity and peace are lacking, our prayers are hindered. The promise is that what we agree to ask will be given to us by our heavenly Father. But too often we pray and pray and are not answered. It is because we do not agree on what we need.

We see that divisions block our prayers and cancel out our sacrifice. *"So if you are offering your gift at the altar and there remember that your brother has something against you, leave your gift there before the altar and go. First be reconciled to your brother, and then come and offer your gift"* (Matt. 5:23-24). So, we see that lack of unity and love stops our specific prayers and devotions.

This is what hindered the prayers and fasting of those in the Bible from finding acceptance (Isa. 58:3). They asked why they fasted and God did not see or take notice of them. He gives this reason: It was because they fasted for strife and debate, and hid their face from their own flesh. Again in Isaiah 59, the Lord says that His hand has not become shorter that he cannot save, nor is his ear deafened that he cannot hear, but their sins had separated God and them. One of the many sins they were charged with was that they had not known the way of peace. Where peace was lacking, prayers were hindered, in the Old and New Testaments.

The sacrifice of the people in Isaiah 65:5 was *"a smoke in my nostrils, a fire that burns all the day."* On the other hand, we read how acceptable those prayers were when they *"lifted their voices together"* (Acts 4:24). They prayed with one accord, and they were all of one heart and one soul. And see the benefit of it: *"they were all filled with the Holy Spirit and continued to speak the word of God with boldness"* (Acts 4:31). This was the very thing they prayed for, as we see in verse 29. And Peter goes on to encourage the husband to live with his wife so that their prayers might not be hindered (1 Peter 3:7). We see that a lack of unity and peace, either in families or churches, is a hindrance to prayers.

Daily Reflection

Although prayer is often seen as an individual part of Christianity, where we speak to God in our personal relationship with Him, there is an important aspect of prayer for the greater body of the church as well. True prayer brings unity and draws us together with the same heart. Prayer meetings are not just another weekly group or opportunity to get together; they are what unites us.

1. When you read Matthew 18:20, do you think God is not there when you pray alone? What is the meaning of this verse then?
2. What hinders prayers when we pray as a group?

3. What is the importance of being aware of our imperfections when we pray?
4. Read Psalm 133:1-3. What does this mean in the context of this chapter?
5. Why is it important to have unity in families as well as in church?

8

GOD'S WAYS OF ANSWERING

"The desire of the righteous will be granted"
—Proverbs 10:24

You might have asked and asked a thousand times on your knees for something, but you still do not have it. Then who was this promise made to?

WE MUST FIRST ASK if the things we desire are good or bad, because a Christian can desire bad things. But let us suppose that what we desire is good and that our hearts are right in asking. Perhaps we desire more grace, yet several things may cause this prayer to not be answered:

1. Even though we desire more of this, we might need to understand the worth of what we are asking for before God will give it to us.
2. What you already have, does it need to be used and perfected?
3. When God gives to His people what they desire, He does it for their advantage:
4. Just before temptation comes; if grace rains down on you, it may be for your advantage. This is like God sending plenty to Egypt just before the years of famine came.
5. Christians often lean too much on their own strength. God sometimes holds back until we are exhausted in our own abilities. We might ask lightly and prize our own works if God did not sometimes deal in this manner with us.
6. It is also to our advantage that we are kept waiting while what we already have is perfected and used. Like the widow who used the flour and oil, she had left before God sent more in abundance.
7. Perhaps we are mistaken. The grace we pray for may have already come. We say we did not receive it, but if we look, it came another way. Understanding the effects of grace, we will be able to see evidence of it already in our lives.
8. Grace brings a convicting light where we see our wickedness even more.
9. Grace breaks the heart because of its wickedness. We fall down before God, ashamed to lift our faces at the sight of how wicked we are.

10. Grace shows us more of the holiness and patience of God; that despite our wickedness, we can come to the throne of grace.
11. Grace is heart-humbling. It will make us put everyone before us and become the lowest.
12. Grace makes us admire other people's characters and actions above ours.
13. More grace brings more surrender and self-denial.

And if we pray for communion with God, it might confuse us instead of comforting us as we see our wickedness. Some people only think they have experienced the presence of God's grace when they are comforted and cheered up.

Hasn't the grace of God been working in you without you knowing? So, therefore your desire is being realized, and when it is accomplished will be sweet to your soul.

1. You say you desire grace and have been on your knees a thousand times before God for more grace, and yet you cannot get it. Why?
2. Maybe the grace which you pray for is worth bringing you to your knees another thousand times more. Waiting for something for a long time makes us better people. So, wait on the Lord. *"Blessed are all those who wait for him"* (Isaiah 30:18).
3. Grace is given for great service. The apostles had to wait for grace to be equipped for the work that was to come. Along with your desire, you will have a reason for it—new work, new trials, new sufferings,

or something that will need the power of grace to keep your spirit steadfast, and your feet from slipping. "*To whom much was given, of him much will be required*" (Luke 12:48). If you desire more grace, also desire wisdom to use it faithfully.
4. Perhaps God withholds what you want so that it might be more valued when it comes. "*Hope deferred makes the heart sick, but a desire fulfilled is a tree of life*" (Prov. 13:12).
5. Do you think having more grace will mean you will be free from temptation? Unfortunately, the more grace you have, the greater the trials.

Grace is the gold of a righteous person. He chooses grace above everything because it makes him more like Jesus and equips him to glorify God in the world.

Daily Reflection

Some people find it very helpful to have a notebook and keep a record of the things that they have asked God for in prayer. When they receive their answers or God gives them what has been asked for, they tick it off. Although a bit like an accounting ledger, it is not so much to keep God accountable but to have a black-and-white reminder of the many times that He actually does come through for us.

1. Has God ever answered your prayer in a way that was different from how you expected?
2. Why does God sometimes withhold his blessings when we ask for them?

3. Have you ever asked for grace? How did God answer?
4. Why do we get frustrated when God decides to make us wait for what we pray for?
5. How much is trust a part of this?

9

THE FEAR OF GOD BRINGS US TO PRAY

"Let us offer to God acceptable worship, with reverence and awe"
—Hebrews 12:28

This reverence or fear is called *"the beginning of wisdom"* (Prov. 9:10) because that is when a person begins to be truly spiritually wise. What wisdom is there when there is no fear of God? (Job 28:28; Psalm 111:10). Therefore, the fools are described as those who *"hated knowledge and did not choose the fear of the Lord"* (Prov. 1:29). The Word of God is the fountain of knowledge into which we cannot look with godly reverence until we have the fear of the Lord. Therefore, it is called *"the beginning of knowledge; fools despise wisdom and instruction"* (Prov. 1:7).

It is this fear of the Lord that makes us wise in our hearts, for life, and heaven. It is this that teaches us how we can escape those spiritual and eternal ruins that the fool falls into and is swallowed up forever. A person who does not have this fear of God, even if they are clever and excel in many things, yet when it comes to the heart, no one is more foolish than them.

This fear, this grace of fear, this son-like fear of God, flows from the love of God to his chosen people. *"I will put the fear of me in their hearts"* (Jer. 32:40). No one else can obtain it but those that are called and chosen by God. They are wrapped up in the everlasting covenant of God and designed to be the people that should be blessed with this fear. "I will make an everlasting covenant with them" saith God, *"that I will not turn away from doing good to them. And I will put the fear of me in their hearts, that they may not turn from me"* (Jer. 32:40).

This fear flows from a new heart. This fear is not in us naturally, except the fear of devils and an ungodly fear of God. But this spiritual fear is not in anyone except those who are born again and have a new heart, another fruit and sign of this everlasting covenant, and this love of God. *"I will give them one heart"* (Jer. 32:39). What heart is that? It is the same one the prophet spoke of: *"a new heart,"* a circumcised one, a sanctified one (Eze. 36:26). So then, until we receive a heart from God, a heart from heaven, a new heart, we do not have this fear of God in us.

What flows from this fear of God is passionate, persistent, and constant prayer. This was also seen in Cornelius, that devoted man. He feared God; and what happened? He gave money to the people and *"prayed continually to God"* (Acts 10:1-2). Lively, passionate, and constant prayer flows from this fear of God, but if that prayer is not managed with this fear of God, it will be useless.

Jesus, *"he was heard because of his reverence"* (Heb. 5:7). He prayed, because He feared, because He feared God, and therefore, His prayer was accepted because He feared—*"he was heard because of his reverence."* This godly fear is so essential to proper prayer, and proper, true prayer is such an inseparable effect and fruit of this fear, that you must have both or none. The person who does not pray does not fear God. The person who does not pray passionately and frequently does not fear Him. The person who does not fear Him, cannot pray, because if prayer is the effect of this fear of God, then without this fear, prayer—fervent prayer—stops.

How can you pray if you do not fear God?

Daily Reflection

Keeping your Bible close by as you work through the chapters is important. Bunyan draws from many scriptures, and it is very good to look them up and read them in their context. Also, you may remember or see a cross-reference to another verse that pertains to what you are reading. This is a good way to conduct a Bible study and see what the Word has to say about the matter.

1. Why is the fear of God so important in prayer?
2. Why is the fear of God the beginning of wisdom?

3. Why is this spiritual fear not natural to us? How do we get it?
4. Does it seem strange that Jesus also had to come to God with reverence?
5. Why is prayer the effect and fruit of reverence?

10

BENEFITS OF PRAYER

"The prayer of a righteous person has great power as it is working"
—James 5:16

Pray often; because prayer is a shield for the soul, a sacrifice to God, and a curse for Satan.

Through prayer, my eyes see clouds lined with silver, like fine clothes; as if I saw the golden face that makes black clouds beautiful with grace. If I compare the sweet incense of prayer to these smoky curled clouds; they seem lined with gold, like prayers that return with abundant blessings.

Prayer is like the jar we use to fetch water from the river so we can water the herbs. Break the jar and it will fetch no water, and without water, the garden withers.

Christians have found many other places, besides the throne of grace, that are empty, that hold no water. They have gone to mount Sinai for help but could find nothing but fire and darkness there, thunder and lightning, earthquakes and trembling, and a voice of words that kill.

They have looked for grace through their own performances; but, unfortunately, they have found nothing but wind and confusion. Every performance, every duty, and every act in any part of religious worship, when looked at through the eyes of the Lord, becomes tarnished and defective.

They have looked for grace through their decisions, their promises, their purposes, and other methods; but they only discover that these are imperfect ways that cannot help them to grace.

They have gone to their tears, their sorrow, and repentance, hoping that they might find some help there; but it has all fled away like the early dew.

They have gone to God as the great Creator, and have seen how wonderful his works are; they have looked to the heavens above, to the earth below, and everything else; but none of these, what they are made of, have given any grace to those who needed it.

They have gone with these jars to their fountains and have returned empty and ashamed; they found no water, no river of water of life.

Paul, not finding it in the law, realizes he will not find it in anything else below, but begins to look for it where he had not yet found it. He looked for it in Jesus Christ, who is the throne of grace. That is where he found it and rejoiced in hope of the glory of God.

When a God of grace is on a throne of grace, and a poor sinner stands near and begs for grace in the name of a gracious Christ, in and by the help of the Spirit of grace, there can be no other result but the sinner obtaining mercy and grace to help in time of need.

All the sorrow and disappointment in our Christianity comes from ourselves, not from the throne of grace. That is the place where our tears are wiped away, and also where we hang up our crutches. The streams that come from the throne of grace are pure and clear, not muddy or frozen, but warm and delightful, and they make the city of God glad.

Daily Reflection

To see prayer as a benefit to our lives is a wonderful revelation, and it frees us from seeing it as just a duty or an obligation that we must perform. The advantages it brings change the way we see our relationship with Jesus and will cause us to grow more in this area of our spiritual lives.

1. How many benefits of prayer can you name?
2. Do you often feel that prayer is simply a condition of Christianity that you must fulfill? Why?
3. Has prayer ever changed your outlook on things? How?
4. What is the result of our decisions, promises, purposes, and other methods?

5. Read Matthew 26:41. What is the benefit of prayer mentioned here?

11

DEALING WITH DISCOURAGEMENTS IN PRAYER

"And let us not grow weary of doing good, for in due season we will reap, if we do not give up"
—Galatians 6:9

Faith is sometimes calm, sometimes up, sometimes down, and sometimes in conflict with sin, death, and the devil. Faith does not always bring peace to the conscience when it is struggling, fighting with angels, with demons; all it can do is cry, groan, sweat, fear, fight, and gasp for life.

I know what it is to go to God for mercy but stand far away because of fear, thinking that God will strike me down to the ground because of my sins. David thought the same thing, so he prayed, *"Cast me not away from your presence, and take not your Holy Spirit from me"* (Psalm 51:11).

Only the person who prays in the Spirit knows what goes up and what is received before the glorious Majesty in prayer.

It is important when praying to God not to go too far or stop too short. Often, we do one or the other. The Pharisee went very far, he was too bold; he came into the temple making such a commotion with his own boasting. He had no thought that he needed a Mediator.

Usually, people who pray try to keep their distance. They are not offensively bold, rushing into the presence of a holy God, especially if they are aware of their own wickedness and sins, like the prodigal son, the lepers, and the poor tax collector. Even Peter, when he suddenly understood the majesty of Jesus his Lord, what did he do? *"He fell down at Jesus' knees, saying, "Depart from me, for I am a sinful man, O Lord"* (Luke 5:8).

When we see God and ourselves, it fills us with a holy fear of how majestic God is, as well as His mercy. What are humans, just dust and ashes, that we should rush in, pushing our way into the presence of the great God?

I sometimes find it one of the hardest things for my soul to do, to come to God, aware that I am a sinner, and share in grace and mercy. It feels to me as if the whole face of heaven were against me. Just thinking of God is too much; I cannot bear it, I cannot stand before Him. I can only say with a thousand tears, *"God, be merciful to me, a sinner!"* (Luke 18:13).

Other times, when my heart is more stubborn and stupid, and I am not afraid, then I can come before Him and ask for His mercy and hardly be aware of sin or grace, or even that I am before God. But those times don't happen often, when I can go to God as the tax collector, aware of God's glorious majesty, aware of my misery, and affectionately cry, "*God, be merciful to me, a sinner!*"

At certain times, even the most righteous person in the world may be overcome by the sin in them, that there is no way to save themselves from a fall but by begging heaven and the throne of grace for help. This is the time when the wandering man that knocked at David's door shall knock at ours; or when we are in the sieve that Satan put Peter in; or when those fists are beating our ears as they did to Paul's; and when that thorn pricks us that Paul said was in his flesh.

Why do the righteous go through these times, except that in them—in their flesh—no good thing exists, only the instinct to follow the devil and his suggestions and lose their soul?

But we have a throne of grace where, as David says, we must continually come, and that is the way to find relief and help in times of need

Daily Reflection

Prayer is not a simple task that we can repeat every day expecting results every time. Sometimes, our own minds get in the way—or more often, our feelings. We can become discouraged because we are unworthy to come to God. Despite the promises He gives us, we want to draw back instead of pushing in. It happens to every Christian no matter how many years they have been born again or how often they pray.

1. Have you ever felt useless or discouraged in your prayers? Why?
2. Do you ever get caught between going too far or stopping too short?
3. Why do you think this happens?
4. Why is the throne of grace the answer to our discouragements?

12

THE PHARISEE'S PRAYER

"The Pharisee, standing by himself, prayed thus: 'God, I thank you that I am not like other men, extortioners, unjust, adulterers, or even like this tax collector. I fast twice a week; I give tithes of all that I get"
—Luke 18:11-12

Pharisees and hypocrites do not like to think of themselves as sinners when they stand before God. They would rather commend themselves as righteous and holy. This is why Jesus told this parable: *"to some who trusted in themselves that they were righteous, and treated others with contempt"* (Luke 18:9). While Moses is read, and his law and the righteousness of it is trusted, a veil is on their heart (2 Cor. 3:14-15). And this is the reason that so many moral people, full of civil and moral righteousness, are so ignorant of themselves and the life of Christ. The Pharisee rested in the law and boasted to God that he was righteous.

We can see by this prayer the strength of self-confidence that can make a person stand before God in a lie, to make them trust in themselves, and boast of their own goodness instead of God's mercy before him. The Pharisee not only justified himself before men but before God.

The Pharisee stands upon a supposed conversion to God—*"I am not like other men"*—but both he and his conversion are rejected at the end of the parable: *"For what is exalted among men is an abomination in the sight of God"* (Luke 16:15). Anything, conversion or people, that flatter themselves is like this. See how this sect, this religion, tricked people and made them worse than they were before (Matt. 23:15). Their doctrine brought only blindness and self-confidence.

By his words, we find the Pharisee not only proclaiming his own conversion but rejoicing in it. *"God, I thank you that I am not like other men."* Thankfully, I am not in the state of sin, death, and judgment as the tax collector is. How deceived to think that a few good works of the flesh are enough to keep your soul before the judgment of God. *"There are those who are clean in their own eyes but are not washed of their filth"* (Prov. 30:12). *"There is a way that seems right to a man, but its end is the way to death"* (Prov. 14:12).

By his words, the Pharisee put his own goodness on the goodness of God. He thanked God when God had done nothing for him; when his way was not God's, but his own. Luther used to say, "In the name of God begins all mischief." Everything is blamed on God.

We also see in this prayer the reason for it; and that is who the Pharisee really was, and what his life was built on. He was not an extortioner, an unjust man, an adulterer, but he fasted twice a week and paid tithes. His foundation was moral and ceremonial, both very thin and weak. Everything he did was good, but only a few inches removed from the most wicked person and their actions; not much to build his confidence for heaven on.

What are a couple of ceremonies, even if they are good? Suppose they are the best and are performed extremely well, they were never meant as a way to get to heaven, and so it is a sandy foundation. But anything will serve as a foundation for some people, and they will use it to support their souls and build their hopes of getting to heaven on it.

I am not a drunk, liar, swearer, or thief, and therefore, I thank God I have hopes of getting to heaven and glory. I am not an extortioner, adulterer, or unjust person like this tax collector, and therefore, I hope to go to heaven.

Doing and having all these things, will it save you from the thunder and fire that the judgment of God places on sin and sinners? No, no, nothing on that day can hide a person from the heat of that vengeance except the righteousness of God, which is not the righteousness of the law, even though it might be called that with any words and phrases that people can invent, for that is just the righteousness of man.

Daily Reflection

We all know the story of the proud Pharisee and the lowly tax collector. The Pharisee is an easy person to point a finger at and see what he did wrong, but it is not as easy to see the same faults, errors, and pride in our own hearts as we pray. By being honest with where we are at, the Holy Spirit will guide us and help us to grow from this place. The first step, though, is to be vulnerable and admit our weaknesses and faults.

1. Why do you think hypocrites do not see that they are wrong when they are before God?
2. What did the Pharisee trust in?
3. Read James 4:6. What do you understand by this?
4. Why are words and actions not important to God? Read 1 Samuel 16:7.
5. In what way do you think you are like the Pharisee?

13

THE TAX COLLECTOR'S PRAYER

"But the tax collector, standing far off, would not even lift up his eyes to heaven, but beat his breast, saying, 'God, be merciful to me, a sinner!'"
—Luke 18:13

First, he confessed: I am a sinner. Second, he begs for help: *"God, be merciful to me, a sinner!"*

For someone to confess they are a sinner is to speak against themselves. We are too much of a hypocrite, a self-flatterer, to confess against ourselves unless we are simple and honest about the conviction in our hearts. He does not say he was or had been but that he *is* a sinner.

In this confession, he judges and condemns himself. It is not enough for someone to confess that they are sinners, but to go on and confess that there is nothing in them, that has been done or can be done by them, that can convince God to do anything for them. We are enemies in our minds; the carnal mind is enmity to God, and that wickedness comes from the wicked.

In this confession, he acknowledges that sin is the worst of things. The Pharisee did not see this, although he may have admitted that at some time or other he had sinned, he never saw what sin was. The right knowledge of sin, in its guilt and filth and terrible power, brings us to understand that nothing but the grace and mercy of Christ can save him from hell.

As a sinner, you might want to say the tax collector's prayer, make the same confession, and say, *"God, be merciful to me, a sinner!"* But do you do it with the tax collector's heart, awareness, dread, and simplicity? If not, you abuse this prayer, yourself, and God. God will reject you and your prayers, saying, "The tax collector I know, his prayers and tears I know; but who are you?"

The tax collector engages and begs for the grace and mercy of God to save him. *"Whoever conceals his transgressions will not prosper, but he who confesses and forsakes them will obtain mercy"* (Prov. 28:13). And again, *"If we confess our sins, he is faithful and just to forgive us our sins and to cleanse us from all unrighteousness"* (1 John 1:9). In the promise of forgiveness, he will find mercy; he will have his sins forgiven.

Solomon also prays that God will forgive them that are aware of the plague of their own heart (2 Chron. 6:29-30; 1 Kings 8:37-38). And the reason is that the sinner is now driven to the farthest point because confession is the farthest point and the utmost place to which God has called the tax collector to go. God says that He does not desire sacrifices or legal righteousness to make us acceptable to Him, but wants us to acknowledge and confess our iniquity that we have transgressed against Him.

And though this may be thought by some to be a very easy thing or place to get to, and to take part in the mercy of God, let the aware sinner try it, and he will find it is one of the hardest things in the world.

Daily Reflection

To see the other side of the parable that Jesus told is to realize the stark contrast between pride and humility. But the tax collector was not simply humble, he was broken with the state of his own heart, and pleaded with God to have mercy on him because of his unbearable sin. Seeing our state before God is one of the best places to be when we come to Him in prayer. It reveals our true need for Him.

1. When you hear the tale of the Pharisee and tax collector, who do you automatically side with? Why?
2. Are you more like the Pharisee or tax collector?
3. Why is confession so important to God, as in 1 John 1:9?
4. What does the confession of our sins bring?
5. What does it mean that God does not require sacrifices? Look at 1 Samuel 15:22.

14

THE POWER OF THE TONGUE

*"For with the heart one believes and is justified,
and with the mouth one confesses and is saved"*
—Romans 10:10

In the parable of the Rich Man and Lazarus, why does it say, let him *"dip the end of his finger in water and cool my tongue"* (Luke 16:24)? Because, like the rest of his body is in sin, every member, including the tongue, is to be punished. Therefore, Jesus is lecturing his disciples not to turn away from Him, but to fear the power of God more than any other power. He said, *"Fear him,"* the one that can send both body and soul to hell (Luke 12:5). And again, *"Fear him who can destroy both soul and body in hell"* (Matt. 10:28).

So, we do not just have only one member, but the whole body, of which the hands, feet, eyes, ears, and tongue are members. And I am sure that while some may say this is just flesh and bones, the truth will be realized, to the misery of those who will have to face God in his just judgment. Then they will cry out, "Give me one small measure of ease for my cursing, swearing, lying, jeering tongue. Some ease for my bragging, braving, flattering, threatening, dissembling tongue!"

Now, we let our tongues do what they want to, or as the saying goes, *"With our tongue we will prevail, our lips are with us; who is master over us?"* (Psalm 12:4). But then, they will think again. Then they will say, "That I might have a little ease for my deceitful tongue." It is a wonder when we see how people let their tongues run at random. It does not seem that they think they will have to give an account for their offending with their tongue. When they think they will have to give an account to Him who is ready to judge the living and the dead, surely they would be more careful of and have more regard for their tongue.

"The tongue," says James, *"is a restless evil, full of deadly poison"*; it sets *"on fire the entire course of life, and set on fire by hell"* (James 3:8, 6). The tongue, how much trouble it can stir up in such a short time! How many injuries and wounds it can cause! How many times, as James says, it can curse people! How many times the tongue brings that hellish poison that is in the heart, both to dishonor God, to hurt neighbors, and to ruin its own soul!

And do you think the Lord will sit still and let your tongue run as it wants, and never bring you to an account for it? No, He will not always keep silent but will discipline you, and bring your sins in order before your eyes. And your tongue, together with the rest of your body parts, will be punished for sinning. And I am very confident that though this might not seem important now, the time is coming when many will regret the day that they ever spoke with their tongue.

Then, they will wish they could bite off their tongue, that they could have been born without a tongue! Right now we are happy to let our tongues say anything for a little profit, for a coin or two. But, what grief this will be on that day when, together with our tongue, we must regret everything that our tongues have done while we were in this world.

If you love your souls, watch your tongues before you tie yourselves so quickly to hell with the sins of your tongues, that you will never be able to get loose again for all eternity. *"By your words you will be condemned,"* if you do not watch and take care of your tongue (Matt. 12:37). For *"I tell you, on the day of judgment people will give account for every careless word they speak"* (Matt. 12:36).

Daily Reflection

Although we often focus on the heart when it comes to judging whether prayer is real or not, it is still that tongue that must speak those words, and often they trip us up—even in prayer! The words we say can land us in judgment if we are not careful. The balance is to make sure that our hearts and mouths are in sync with each other, speaking to God in spirit and truth.

1. Read James 1:26. What does this verse mean?
2. How does this verse relate to prayer?
3. Read Psalm 19:14 and see how closely the heart and mouth are linked in times of devotion and prayer.
4. Read Matthew 12:37. Why does Jesus say this?

15

UNANSWERED PRAYERS

"As I called, and they would not hear, so they called, and I would not hear," says the Lord of hosts"
—Zechariah 7:13

Prayers that are not answered are ones that are presented to God in their own strength, without Jesus. Even though God has appointed prayer, and promised to hear our prayers, he will not accept the prayer of anyone who does not come in Christ. *"And whatever you do, in word or deed, do everything in the name of the Lord Jesus"* (Col. 3:17). *"If you ask me anything in my name"* (John 14:14). Even though you are devoted, passionate, sincere, and constant in prayer, it is only in Christ that you will be heard and accepted.

Most people do not know what it is to come to Him in the name of the Lord Jesus, which is why they live wicked, pray wicked, and also die wicked. Or else, they succeed in nothing else but what normal people succeed in doing, to be able to express themselves in word and action between people, and only with the righteousness of the law appear before God.

Another thing that blocks prayer is the form of it without the power. It is an easy thing for us to be very passionate about the format of prayers, as they are written in a book, but we forget to ask whether we have the spirit and power of prayer. This is like being a hollow person with prayers, like a false voice. We appear as hypocrites and our prayers are an abomination (Prov. 28:9).

When we say we have been pouring out our hearts to God, He says we have been howling like dogs (Hosea 7:14). So, when we intend to pray to the Lord of heaven and earth, consider these:

1. Seriously consider what you want. Do not beat the air and ask for things you do not desire or need.
2. When you see what you want, stick to that and make sure you pray sensibly. If you are not sure, then it is best not to pray at all. If you find you have no idea, but you are aware of that, then according to your awareness, if you need anything, pray. And if you are aware that you have no clear idea, pray for the Lord to make you aware of whatever does not make sense in your heart. This was the practice of prominent men of God.

- "*Lord, make me know my end,*" cries David (Psalm 39:4).
- And to this is added the promise, "*Call to me and I will answer you, and will tell you great and hidden things that you have not known*" (Jer. 33:3).

Make sure that your heart goes to God as well as your mouth. Do not let your mouth go any further than your heart. David would lift his heart and soul to the Lord, because when a person's mouth goes along without his heart, then it only becomes lip service. So, if you want to go further in prayer before God, see that it is with your heart.

If you are passionate in your words, make sure it is not just to please yourself that you forget the life of prayer.

Do not stop praying because you feel that you do not have the Spirit. It is the great work of the devil to do his best, or rather worst, against the best prayers. He will flatter hypocrites and feed them with a thousand thoughts of doing well, when their duties of prayer, and everything else, stink in the nostrils of God. The devil will stand near Joshua to resist him and persuade him that neither his person nor performances are accepted by God (Isa. 65:5; Zech. 3:1).

So, watch out for these false conclusions and groundless discouragements. Even though you feel them, do not be discouraged by them, but use them to make you even more sincere and eager to approach God. In the same way, do not let your own heart's deceptions stop you. You may find all those things mentioned before and feel many things that are making it hard to carry on praying to Him. Your job is to judge these feelings and deceptions, to pray against them, and to bring yourself even more before the feet of God, in a sense of your own wickedness. Rather than making an argument from your wickedness and corruption of heart, plead with God for justifying and sanctifying grace rather than an argument of discouragement and despair. David did this when he said, *"For your name's sake, O Lord, pardon my guilt, for it is great"* (Psalm 25:11).

Daily Reflection

Dealing with unanswered prayers is one of the biggest struggles that Christians go through. It happens to every believer at some point, no matter how far along in their Christian journey they are. Trying to understand why is often hard, and sometimes, as in the end, it is up to God to decide how and when to answer. But Bunyan gives some good advice as he looks at this issue.

1. What does it mean to come to Him in the name of the Lord Jesus?
2. Read 2 Timothy 3:5 concerning this chapter. What does it mean?
3. Have you ever felt discouraged and wanted to give up praying? Why?
4. Why is the devil intent on discouraging prayer?
5. Have you ever had unanswered prayers? What were they?

16

PRAYING WITHOUT THE SPIRIT

"In all circumstances take up the shield of faith, with which you can extinguish all the flaming darts of the evil one; and take the helmet of salvation, and the sword of the Spirit, which is the word of God, praying at all times in the Spirit, with all prayer and supplication"
—Ephesians 6:16-18

There are people who mock and undervalue the Spirit and praying in the Spirit. It would be counted as high treason to speak against a king, and yet they blaspheme the Spirit of the Lord.

Did God send his Holy Spirit into the hearts of his people, and you will mock that? You might be concerned about being judged for your sins against the law, but you still sin against the Holy Spirit. Must the holy and pure Spirit of grace, the nature of God, the promise of Christ, the Comforter of his children, that without which no one can do anything acceptable to the Father—is this the one you mock?

If God sent Korah and his company to hell for speaking against Moses and Aaron, do you think you will escape unpunished for mocking the Spirit? (Num. 16; Heb. 10:29). Did you not read what God did to Ananias and Sapphira for telling a lie against it? (Acts 5:1-8). Also to Simon Magus for undervaluing it? (Acts 8:18-22). It is a terrible thing to do to the Spirit of grace (Compare Matt. 12:31 with Mark 3:28-30).

Do not resist the Spirit of prayer because someone has invented a story against it. A twist of the devil can make the traditions of men seem better than the Spirit of prayer. This is the same as what Jeroboam did, keeping many from going to Jerusalem, the place of God's worship. As a result, God was not pleased with him until this day (1 Kings 12:26-33).

You would think that God's judgments on the hypocrites in the Bible would make us take notice and be afraid to do the same. Yet many teachers and professors ignore the warning of the punishment of others and rush into the same transgression, setting up a man-made institution that is not commanded or commended by God. Whoever disobeys God like this should be driven either out of the land or the world.

Because of the traditions of men, the Spirit of prayer is disowned, and the form imposed; the Spirit devalued, and the form exalted. Those people who pray with the Spirit, even though they are humble and holy, are counted as fanatics. And those people who pray with a set format, and nothing else, are seen as righteous! How will those who see it like this answer the verse in the Bible that tells the church to turn away from anything *"having the appearance of godliness, but denying its power"*? (2 Tim. 3:5).

If we had to compare a form of prayer made by men with the spirit of prayer, it would not take long to prove which one is which. Because the person who respects a prayer book above the Spirit of prayer approves of man-made things above the Spirit. But this is what those people who try to do away with the Spirit of prayer are doing. They hug and embrace those who pray only by format because they do the same. Therefore, they love and advance the form of prayers over and above the Spirit of prayer, which is God's special and gracious appointment.

Lifting up a prayer book above praying by the Spirit or preaching the Word has no godliness in it. May the Lord, in His mercy, turn the hearts of people to seek more after the Spirit of prayer, and in the strength of that, to pour out their souls before Him.

Daily Reflection

As we have already learned from previous chapters, praying in the Spirit is very important. Without Him, our prayers are useless before God. But so often, we end up doing things in our own strength or find formats and rituals easier to accomplish than trying to understand which way the Holy Spirit moves. We must see the biblical directive and advantage of praying in the Spirit.

1. Do you know anyone who does not agree with the Spirit's guidance in our lives? What is their view?
2. Why is the Spirit so important in prayer?
3. Look at Romans 8:26-27 in answering question 2.
4. Do you think there is any use for written prayers and prayer books?
5. Read Ephesians 6:18-20 and see what it says about *when* we should pray in the Spirit.

17

A PRAYER TOO LATE

"For he says, 'In a favorable time I listened to you, and in a day of salvation I have helped you.' Behold, now is the favorable time; behold, now is the day of salvation"
—2 Corinthians 6:2

What a change it will be when a person reaches hell. The rich man in the parable of Lazarus *"called out"* (Luke 16:24). It is like he was laughing, joking, drinking, mocking, swearing, cursing, and persecuting the Christians, among his bad companions. But now the case is reversed, now he is in another state of attitude, now his proud, stubborn appearance has vanished. '*And he called out.*' The laughter of the ungodly will not always last, but will surely end in a cry; *"the exulting of the wicked is short"* (Job 20:5).

When you think about it like this, you must either change here or in hell. If you are born again in this lifetime before you die, your attitude will be changed, your conditions will be changed; but if not, you will end up in hell and cry. The devil works hard to get people to follow their sins, he works hard to keep thoughts of eternal damnation out of their minds. These two things are so closely linked together that the devil cannot get someone to happily carry on in sin unless he can keep the thoughts of that terrible judgment day out of their minds.

What a change there will be among the ungodly when they leave this world. It may be a week or a month before their departure; they were light, happy, surly, drinking themselves drunk, mocking Christians, laughing at goodness, loving their sin, following the world, and seeking after riches, but now, they are dropped down into hell, they cry. A little while ago they were painting their faces, feeding their lusts, chasing women, robbing their neighbors, telling lies, and following entertainment and sports to pass the time.

Now, they are in hell, and why do they cry?

1. They will cry out because they are cut off from the land of the living, never to be there again.
2. They will cry out because the gospel of Christ was so freely offered, and yet they did not take advantage of it.
3. They will cry out realizing that the chance to repent and be saved, even though they might not accept it, is gone.

4. They will cry out because they were so foolish to follow their pleasures when others were following Jesus (Luke 13:28).
5. They will cry out because they are separated from God, Jesus, and the kingdom of heaven forever.
6. Because their crying will do them no good now.
7. Because they must stand on the left hand of Jesus, among the condemned on the day of judgment.
8. They will cry out because Lazarus, whom they mocked, will sit with Jesus and pass a sentence of condemnation on their souls (1 Cor. 6:2-3).
9. They will cry because when the judgment is over, and others go to the kingdom of glory, they must go back into that dungeon of darkness and be tormented for as long as eternity lasts.

Is it not better to leave sin, and come to Jesus, even though it means giving up this world of pleasures and feeding your lusts? Do not wait and put off the cry and prayer for the grace of Jesus.

Daily Reflection

The story of Lazarus and the rich man is a very sobering parable about hell and heaven. It's one of the only real glimpses we are given of the difference between where people will go after they die and what they will endure. In looking at the rich man's cry for help, we can see that while we are on this side of eternal life, our own prayers and cries for help are not for nothing.

1. Do you know people who have died without acknowledging or receiving Jesus into their lives? What do you think about that?
2. Does this move your heart for the lost, to pray for those who do not know Jesus yet?
3. Does this story have any relation to us who already know Jesus as our personal savior?
4. Why do you think 2 Corinthians 6:2 calls it the "favorable time" to call out to God?

18

CENSERS OF PRAYER

"And another angel came and stood at the altar with a golden censer, and he was given much incense to offer with the prayers of all the saints on the golden altar before the throne"
—Revelation 8:3

The censers were for use in the temple to hold the holy fire, on which incense was to be burned before the Lord (Lev. 10:1-2). These censers are like hearts. Aaron's golden one is Jesus' golden heart, and the censers of the Levites are the other worshippers' hearts. The fire is the Spirit by which we pray, and the incense that is burnt is our desires.

Of Jesus' censer we read in Revelation 8 that it is always filled with incense—continual intercessions, which he offers to God for us; and a cloud of sweet savor, covering the mercy seat, always comes from it (Lev. 16:13; Heb. 7:25; Rev. 8:3-4).

For us, a golden censer is a gracious heart, heavenly fire is the Holy Spirit, and sweet incense is the effective, passionate prayer of faith. Have you got these? God expects them, and you must have them if you and your performances are to be accepted by God.

But not all the censers, fire, and incense of the worshippers are pure and holy:

1. Two hundred and fifty censers that Korah and his company offered are called the censers of sinners because they came with wicked hearts to burn incense before the Lord (Num. 16:17, 37).
2. As the censers of these men were called the censers of sinners, because they came to God with proud, wicked hearts, so the fire that was in Nadab and Abihu's censers is called strange fire, which the Lord commanded them not to bring (Lev. 10:1).
3. This strange fire is the strange spirit opposed to the Spirit of God, that some try to worship God with.
4. As these censers are called the censers of sinners, and this fire called strange fire, so the incense of it is also called strange, and is an abomination to God (Exo. 30:9; Isa. 1:13, 66:3).

So, you see that both the censers, fire, and incense of some are rejected, even as the heart, spirit, and prayer of sinners are an abomination to God (Hosea 7:14, 4:12, 5:4; Prov. 28:9).

But there were also true censers, holy fire, and sweet incense among the worshippers in the temple, and their service was accepted by Aaron, their high priest. It was through the faith of Jesus, and these are our true gospel worshippers, who come with holy hearts, a holy spirit, and holy desires before God, our Redeemer. These are a perfume in his nose. *"The prayer of the upright is acceptable to him"* (Prov. 15:8). Their prayers went up like *"incense before you, and the lifting up of my hands as the evening sacrifice!* (Psalm 141:2).

Let those who pretend to worship before God in his holy temple make sure that their censers, fire, incense, heart, spirit, and desires are as the word requires. Otherwise, instead of receiving blessings and favor from God, their censers will be held against them, the fire of God will devour them, and their incense will become an abomination to him, as it happened to those mentioned before.

This is God's worship, by his command, yet even that worship can be spoiled by our transgression. Prayer is God's command, but all prayer is not accepted by God. We must distinguish between what is commanded, and how we use and apply it. The temple was God's house but was abused by the irreverence of those who worshiped there.

Daily Reflection

John Bunyan wrote a lot about the tabernacle, the temple, and the holy of holies. In his writings, he looked at each part of the ancient priestly duties and how these relate to us in a spiritual sense today. We can learn much through these teachings and see the aspects of the Old Covenant as a picture of what we enjoy and share in the New Covenant. To learn more about these, you can read Charles Spurgeon's sermons on the temple and tabernacle.

1. What do you understand by the censer as an image of worship and prayer?
2. What is meant by "strange fire" in Leviticus 10? What is it in our lives?
3. Why does God hate this "strange fire" so much?
4. What kind of prayer and worship does God not accept?
5. Read Romans 12:1-2 and see what God calls acceptable.

19

ALTAR OF INCENSE

*"Let my prayer be counted as incense before you,
and the lifting up of my hands as the evening sacrifice!"*
—Psalm 141:2

The altar of incense was set before the veil before entering the holiest part. When the priest went in to make an atonement, he was to take fire from off that altar to burn his incense within the holy place (Exodus 30:1-10; Lev. 16:18).

1. It was called the golden altar because it was covered with pure gold. This altar was not for burnt-offering, the meat-offering, or the drink-offering, but to burn incense (Exodus 30:7). This sweet incense was a type of grace and prayer (Psalm 112:2).

2. Incense was a compound made up of sweet spices called stacte, onycha, and galbanum. They can be likened to these three parts of this duty: prayer, supplication, and intercession (Exodus 30:34-37, 37:29; 1 Tim. 2:1).
3. This incense was to be burned on the altar every morning before the veil to show that it is our duty every morning to make our prayer to God by Jesus Christ before the veil—the door of heaven, where we seek, knock, and ask for what we need, according to the Bible (Luke 11:9-13).
4. This incense was to be kindled every morning, to show how Jesus continues interceding for us, and also that all true praise is by the renewing of the Holy Spirit in our hearts (Rom. 8:26).
5. Incense was to burn and give off smoke to show that the prayer that flows from the spirit of faith and grace is not cold and flat, but hot and passionate (Zech. 12:10; Jer. 5:16).
6. The smoke of this incense was very sweet and savory, like pleasant perfume, to show how delightful and acceptable the very sound and noise of proper prayer is to the nostrils of the living God because it comes from a broken heart (Psalm 51:17).
7. This incense was to be offered on the golden altar to show us that no prayer is accepted except what is directed to God in the name of His Son our Savior (1 Peter 2:5; Heb. 13:15).
8. They were commanded to burn incense every morning on this altar, to show that God is never tired of the righteous prayers of his people. It also shows

that we need to go to God every day for fresh supplies of grace to carry us through this evil world.
9. This altar is to teach us to live by faith and to make use of the name of Jesus. We find it in the temple so close to the holiest place that the smell of the smoke might go in to show that no distance can keep the voice of true prayer from our God. He will hear what we ask for according to his word. This is why it says, *"it is good to be near God"* (Psalm 73:28; Heb. 10:22).
10. This altar was placed before the ark within the veil to remind us that the law cannot hurt us; to let us know that the mercy seat is above and that God sits there with grace to save us. When the priest approached the altar with incense in the right way, it pleased God. How much more will ourselves and our prayers be accepted, and given what we need, if we come as we should to God by Jesus Christ?

Be sure you do not approach a wrong altar; be sure that you come not with strange fire; for they are dangerous things, and cause us to miss out on what we should enjoy.

Daily Reflection

This is another aspect of the tabernacle and temple that Bunyan writes about, and is especially related to prayer. Often we hear or speak of incense as our prayers that are lifting up before God to be a sweet-smelling fragrance to Him. This is a wonderful picture of how we all want our prayers to be to the Lord. Understanding a bit of the actual importance and function of this part of the Old Testament temple can open our eyes to see the importance and beauty of prayer today.

1. Why is incense such a fitting picture of prayer?
2. Why do you think there were such strict rules for the rituals to be followed in temple days?
3. What kind of prayer is not acceptable to God?
4. What is the holy of holies? Why is it possible for us to enter now when the priests were not allowed to? See Hebrews 10:19.
5. Read Ephesians 5:1-2. How does this relate to our prayers in this sense?

20

PRAY FOR YOUR MIND AND WILL

*"Set your minds on things that are above,
not on things that are on earth"*
—Colossians 3:2

Plead with God to open your eyes and your mind.

One of the reasons why men and women have little regard for heaven is because they see so little of it. This is why Paul said that we should *"no longer walk as the Gentiles do, in the futility of their minds. They are darkened in their understanding, alienated from the life of God because of the ignorance that is in them, due to their hardness of heart"* (Eph. 4:17-18). Do not walk like them.

When we see God, Jesus, heaven, and the eternal glory there is to be enjoyed, we will run through thick and thin to enjoy it. This is what Paul often prayed for in his letters to the churches: *"That you may know what is the hope to which he has called you, what are the riches of his glorious inheritance in the saints"* (Eph. 1:18). And that they might *"comprehend with all the saints what is the breadth and length and height and depth, and to know the love of Christ that surpasses knowledge"* (Eph. 3:18-19).

So, pray that God will open your eyes and mind because it will help you. It will help you endure many hardships for Jesus; as Paul says, *"after you were enlightened, you endured a hard struggle with sufferings, sometimes being publicly exposed to reproach and affliction, and sometimes being partners with those so treated. For you had compassion on those in prison, and you joyfully accepted the plundering of your property, since you knew that you yourselves had a better possession and an abiding one"* (Heb. 10:32-34). If a rare jewel lies in your way, but you do not see it, you will walk over it and not pick it up.

So, pray to the Lord for enlightening grace, and say, "Lord, open my blind eyes. Lord, take the veil off my dark heart, show me the things of heaven, and let me see its glory."

Pray to God that he will set your will after heaven. When your will is set to do something, then it is hard to stop you from getting there. When Paul's will was set to go to Jerusalem, even though he knew he would suffer, he was not put off. Instead, he said, *"I am ready not only to be imprisoned but even to die in Jerusalem for the name of the Lord Jesus"* (Acts 21:13). His will was filled with love for Jesus, and therefore, all the persuasions against going came to nothing.

No one knows what to do with strong self-willed people—they will have their own will, no matter what you do. To have such a strong will for heaven is a great advantage for us if we choose to run in that direction. We will be resolved, and if our will is fixed, we can say, "I will do my best to give myself every advantage and to stop my enemies from diverting me. I will not give up as long as I can stand. I will have it or I will lose my life." *"Though he slay me, I will hope in him"* (Job 13:15). *"I will not let you go unless you bless me"* (Gen. 32:26).

I WILL, I WILL, I WILL! This is the strong, determined will for heaven! What is like it? If you are willing, then any argument against it will only become an encouragement, but if you are unwilling, then any argument will just discourage you.

So, ask God to open your mind and set your will on heaven.

Daily Reflection

There are two things that often come into conflict with our heart and spirit when we want to pray or do things for the Lord: our mind and our will. They are both very strong and we often follow them quicker than obeying the still voice of the Holy Spirit. Learning to bring these under God's command will allow us to enter into spiritual prayer that will realize many benefits and much fruit.

1. Why is our mind and will so strong, often against the will of God?
2. Why does Bunyan put so much emphasis on being able to see God, Jesus, and heaven as one of the ways to overcome our fleshly minds?

3. What does being 'enlightened' mean in this context?
4. Do you think Paul's outlook in Acts 21:13 was a little drastic or radical?
5. Do you find it difficult to allow Jesus to bring your will and mind under control?

21

COMMITTING YOUR SOUL TO GOD

"Therefore let those who suffer according to God's will entrust their souls to a faithful Creator while doing good.
—1 Peter 4:19

To entrust your soul to God is to carry it to Him, to lift it to Him, on bended knees, and to pray for Jesus to take it into his care, and to let it be kept by Him. Also, that He will deliver it from all those traps that are laid for it, and that He will see that it is safe and sound at the judgment, even though so many are against you.

David committed his soul to God when he said *"Arise, O LORD! Confront him, subdue him! Deliver my soul from the wicked by your sword"* (Psalm 17:13). And again, *"Be pleased, O LORD, to deliver me! O LORD, make haste to help me! Let those be put to shame and disappointed altogether who seek to snatch away my life"* (Psalm 40:13-14).

This is what it is to commit the soul to God. This is what Peter is telling the sufferers to do, to carry their soul to God and leave it with him while they live for His name in the world.

God has enough power for those who have laid their soul at his foot to be preserved. He is called the soul keeper, the soul-preserver (Prov. 24:12). *"The LORD is your keeper; the LORD is your shade on your right hand. The sun shall not strike you by day, nor the moon by night. The LORD will keep you from all evil; he will keep your life"* (Psalm 121:5-7). You will be kept and preserved, carried through and delivered from all evil. So, commit the keeping of your soul to Him, if you are suffering and would have it secured and found safe and sound at last.

1. Then your natural weakness and timidity will not overcome you. God can make the most soft-spirited man as hard as steel. If God takes care of his soul, He can fit him with brass, and give him hooves of iron (Deut. 33:25). There is nothing too hard for God. He can say to you, *"Be strong; fear not!"* (Isa. 35:4). He can say, Let the weak say I am strong (Zech. 12:8).
2. Your natural ignorance will not cause you to fall. He *"chose what is foolish in the world to shame the wise"* (1 Cor. 1:27). Wisdom and might are His, He can give you the Spirit of wisdom and revelation in the knowledge of his Son (Eph. 1:17). He promised to do it so that those committed to Him will overcome those that oppose them. He said He *"'will give you a*

mouth and wisdom, which none of your adversaries will be able to withstand or contradict" (Luke 21:15).
3. Your doubts He can dissolve, crush, and bring to nothing. He can make fear flee far away and place heavenly confidence in its place. The Spirit of glory and of God rests on those who suffer for the name of Jesus (1 Peter 4:14).

"I can do all things," said Paul, *"through him who strengthens me"* (Phil. 4:13). And again, I take pleasure in infirmities, in reproaches, in necessities, in persecutions, in distresses for Christ's sake (2 Cor. 12:10). But how can that be, since no suffering when it happens at the time seems enjoyable or good? I answer though they might not feel like it, but Christ, by His presence, can make them good, because then His power rests on us. When I am weak, then I am strong; then Jesus does mighty things in me because my strength is made perfect in weakness; in affliction, for the gospel's sake.

Daily Reflection

In your daily reflections, it is also good to allow time to discuss the topics or questions with others and to get feedback or other points of view. Even being vulnerable about things you struggle with or are still trying to understand can be good. Speaking with those who are grounded and solid in their own faith is good, as it will ensure that you stay close to the biblical truths of what is being taught and not simply entertain people's ideas and opinions.

1. What does it mean to commit your soul to God, as in this chapter?
2. Why is it important to do this on a regular basis?
3. What are the benefits of committing your soul to God?
4. What are the three natural aspects that committing your soul overcomes?
5. What is the relation of Philippians 4:13 in this context?

22

CLOSET SIN

"But when you pray, go into your room and shut the door and pray to your Father who is in secret. And your Father who sees in secret will reward you"
—Matthew 6:6

Those who call themselves Christians and profess the name of Jesus should turn away from the sins of their closet. These could be called sins of the house or private sins because it is not something public. There are many closet sins that Christians might be guilty of, and from which they need to depart.

1. There is pride in a library or the study. I doubt that many Christians think this would be called a sin, but it is. People will secretly be pleased with themselves

thinking of the collection of books they have or when they take more pleasure in how many they have rather than the matter contained in their books. Sometimes they buy books to increase the number of books rather than to learn to be good and godly men from them. And even though they own these books to help them be good and righteous, they do not conform to or follow their teachings. This is a sin that is becoming more prevalent and needs to be avoided. It is better to have no books and stay away from the iniquity of pride than to have a thousand and not to learn or grow from them.

2. There is a sin that has to do with the closet, but not what is in it; rather, it is a vacancy in the closet. When people have a closet to talk of, not to pray in; a closet to look at, not to kneel before God in; a closet to store gold in, but not to mourn in for the sins of their life; a closet that if it could speak, would say, "My owner is seldom here on his knees before God; hardly ever here humbling himself for the iniquity of his heart, or to thank God for the blessings in his life."

3. Some people are guilty of closet sins when they do not completely neglect their Christian duties, but they perform them formally, in their own efforts, without reverence or the Spirit. Also, when they ask God for things that they cannot or do not follow or look after. Or when they pray for those things in his closet that they cannot follow or tolerate in his house, or his life.

4. There are those who are guilty of closet sins when they love to have the sound of their devotion and prayer heard in the house, the street, or the neighborhood. A closet or prayer room is only for that person and God to do things in secret (Matt. 6:6).

These things Christians must beware of so that they do not add more sin until they are rejected and turned away by God. The closet is appointed by God for us to wait on Him in, and to do it without hypocrisy; to wait there for His mind and His will, and also for His grace to do His will. If I see sin in my heart, the Lord will not hear my prayer, and will not meet me in my closet. If so, then we must quickly be careful and watch out for our pride.

It is a great thing to be a "closet Christian." A close Christian is a closet Christian. When I say a closet Christian, I mean someone who is a Christian outward as well as deep in the hidden part of their heart, and who also walks with God, not someone who hides what they really are. Many admit to following Jesus, but they are more often in the coffee shop than in their closet. They will rather spend time in a morning run than praying to God and beginning the day with Him. But for you who call yourself a Christian, depart from all these things.

Read and practice what you read. Follow after righteousness. Begin the day with God, because the person who does not begin it with Him will hardly end it with Him. The person who runs from God in the morning will hardly find him at the end of the day. The person who starts the day with the world and its pleasures will not be very capable of walking with God throughout the rest of the day. Only the person who finds God in their closet will carry the fragrance of Him into their house, shop, and conversations. When Moses had been with God on the mountain, his face shone, and he brought that glory back into the camp (Exodus 34).

Daily Reflection

These days, coming out of the closet has many negative connotations. But the closet was often the term for a prayer room or a place you could go and be alone with God on your own, and in private. It, therefore, means who you are in your private and personal capacity, worshiping and praying before the Lord.

1. What are the different closet sins in the context of this chapter?
2. Why do you think we fall into these kinds of traps and end up in sin?
3. Why do you think God does not reward those who pray in public but rather those who do so in private, according to Matthew 6:6?
4. Do you find it easier to pray in public or in private, on your own with God?
5. Bunyan hits hard when he talks about coffee shops and morning runs instead of spending time in prayer. Are you guilty of any of these?

23

PRAYER OF A BROKEN HEART

*"The sacrifices of God are a broken spirit;
a broken and contrite heart, O God, you will not despise"*
—Psalm 51:17

A broken spirit and a contrite heart recognize a sense of sin, and not only brings us to hate it but also ourselves because of it. It also brings sorrowful mourning to God because we know that our soul has insulted and disregarded both God and his holy Word.

This kind of heart will bring prayers and tears for mercy as we desire not to be in love with sin but to be firmly joined and knitted to God in our souls. From Satan to God, from sin to grace, from death to life, we have scattered with tears and prayers, with weeping and supplication. We will go weeping and seeking the Lord our God.

We become strangers and pilgrims, not ashamed to declare that there is nothing in this world under the sun or on this side of heaven that can satisfy the longings, the desire, and cravings of a broken heart and a contrite spirit.

If a broken heart and a contrite spirit are so treasured by God, then this should encourage those who have it to come to God with it. I know the great encouragement for us to come to God is that there *"is one mediator between God and men, the man Christ Jesus"* (1 Tim. 2:5). This is the best encouragement, and there is none that can take its place, but there are other encouragements, and a broken heart and a contrite spirit are one of them—evident in several places in the Bible.

If you cannot carry a broken heart and a sorrowful spirit with you when you go to God, tell Him your heart is wounded inside, that you have sorrow in your heart and are sorry for your sins. Confess your sins to Him and tell Him they are always before you. David made an argument about these things when he went to God in prayer. He said, *"O Lord, rebuke me not in your anger, nor discipline me in your wrath!"* (Psalm 38:1). Why did he say this?

David continues, *"For my iniquities have gone over my head; like a heavy burden, they are too heavy for me... I am utterly bowed down and prostrate; all the day I go about mourning... I am feeble and crushed; I groan because of the tumult of my heart. O Lord, all my longing is before you; my sighing is not hidden from you"* (Psalm 38:4-9).

These are the words, sighs, complaints, prayers, and arguments of a broken heart to God for mercy. *"Have mercy on me, O God, according to your steadfast love; according to your abundant mercy blot out my transgressions. Wash me thoroughly from my iniquity, and cleanse me from my sin! For I know my transgressions, and my sin is ever before me"* (Psalm 51:1-3).

God allows people who can, without lying, to plead and argue with him. *"But I am afflicted and in pain"* said the good man to Him, *"let your salvation, O God, set me on high!"* (Psalm 69:29). If you have a broken heart, have courage, God tells you to have courage. Ask your soul, *"Why are you cast down, O my soul, and why are you in turmoil within me? Hope in God"* (Psalm 43:5).

But sometimes the brokenhearted are far from this; they faint. They think God will no longer remember them—the greatness of God, his holiness, and their own sins and wickedness will certainly consume them. They feel guilt and anguish in their souls; they go mourning the whole day; their mouth is full of gravel. Who can come to God under this guilt, and plead in faith that the sacrifices of God are a broken heart and that "a broken and a contrite spirit God will not despise"? God will certainly reject someone who comes to him without a broken heart.

Come broken, come contrite, come aware of and sorry for your sins, or your coming will not be right before God.

Daily Reflection

Nobody really wants to have a broken heart and suffer through the pain of it, and yet that is what we need to have and bring to God as sacrifices. Too often, we confuse our understanding of an emotionally 'broken' heart with the real spiritual meaning of what it is to be contrite and humbled. In prayer, this is how the Lord wants us to come, and these are the prayers that He hears the most!

1. Why are a broken spirit and a contrite heart acceptable sacrifices to God?
2. Why do you think God is pleased when we are aware and sorry for our sinful state?
3. How does this compare with James 4:6?
4. Why do you think God allows people to plead and argue with Him?
5. Read Psalm 34:18 as an encouragement for when you find yourself brokenhearted.

24

A HIGH PRIEST WHO INTERCEDES

"Christ Jesus is the one who died—more than that, who was raised—who is at the right hand of God, who indeed is interceding for us"
—Romans 8:34

A person in court, through intercession, gets a pardon for another person. That second person knows that his pardon was gained by the other's interceding, even though he may be ignorant about the method of intercession. It is the same with us and Jesus. We should believe that for Jesus' sake, God will save me since He has justified me with His blood; *"therefore, we have now been justified by his blood, much more shall we be saved by him from the wrath of God"* (Rom. 5:9). Through his intercession, or his coming between God and me, His blood was shed for me, and those merits are made mine by an act of God's grace, according to His eternal covenant made with Jesus. This is how He makes intercession.

Imagine Jesus stood before the Father sitting on a throne, presented His merits, and made vocal prayers for the life and salvation of His people.

See here how He is qualified: He was tempted as we are, suffered temptations as we do, in everything as we are; that He might be a merciful and faithful High Priest, in things pertaining to God, to make up the difference that is made by sin between God and His people, to make reconciliation for the sins of the people. *"Therefore he had to be made like his brothers in every respect, so that he might become a merciful and faithful high priest in the service of God, to make propitiation for the sins of the people. For because he himself has suffered when tempted, he is able to help those who are being tempted"* (Heb. 2:17-18).

We are also His members, part of His body. So, Jesus makes intercession for himself, for his own body, and the members of His body. The High Priest under the law offered a sacrifice first for his own sins, and then for the errors of the people. Jesus had no sin, but He made the sins of the people His own (Psalm 69:5). God the Father made us His. We are the ones who He forever lives to make intercession for; we are united to Him, made members of His body, of His flesh, and His bones; we are part of Him (2 Cor. 5:21).

Because we are part of Him, He must care for us; the weaker we are, the more He is touched by our weaknesses: *"For we do not have a high priest who is unable to sympathize with our weaknesses"* (Heb. 4:15). Who would not make many supplications, prayers, and intercessions for a weak leg, for an injured eye, a foot, a hand, a finger, rather than losing it? If Jesus loses a member, he would be disfigured, maimed, and dismembered. For his body is called His fullness.

Our High Priest is not like the ones you read of in the law (Lev. 21:18). He has no sin or imperfection, therefore will not fail to fulfill His duties, but is able to save those who come to God by Him, *"since he always lives to make intercession for them"* (Heb. 7:25). And it is also worth noting that He is appointed, instituted, called, and qualified by God; this shows the Father's heart, as well as the Son's, to us, that this priesthood was of Him. *"Let us then with confidence draw near to the throne of grace, that we may receive mercy and find grace to help in time of need"* (Heb. 4:16).

Believe that Christ died, was buried, rose again, ascended, and lives forever to make intercession for you.

Daily Reflection

As Bunyan wrote about the temple and tabernacle so much, it was almost inevitable that he would include descriptions and teachings about the High Priest. But more significant than the role of the priest in the Old Testament is how Jesus fulfills that duty for us in the New Covenant. It is even more important considering that He is the one who intercedes and stands before God on our account. When it comes to prayer, this makes a huge difference to the way we should approach prayer and expect our prayers to be heard.

1. Can you describe, in your own words, what intercession means?

2. Why do we need a High Priest to intercede for us?
3. What qualifies Jesus to take on this role on behalf of us humans?
4. Does knowing that Jesus is always interceding for us make a difference in the way you pray?
5. What is the relation between Jesus' jobs as advocate and priest? See 1 John 2:1.

25

CRYING OUT TO GOD

"Out of the depths I cry to you, O Lord! O Lord, hear my voice! Let your ears be attentive to the voice of my pleas for mercy!"
—Psalm 130:1-2

One sign of a broken heart is crying, a crying out. Pain will make a person cry. Go to someone who has broken bones and see if they do not cry. Anguish makes them cry. This is what happens once your heart is broken, and your spirit is made contrite.

Anguish will make you cry. *"Trouble and anguish have found me out"* (Psalm 119:143). Anguish naturally provokes crying. Just as a broken bone has anguish, a broken heart has anguish. So, the pain of a person that has a broken heart is compared to that of a woman in labor (John 16:20-22).

Anguish will make you cry alone, to yourself. This is called grieving and lamenting. *"I have heard Ephraim grieving,"* said God (Jer. 31:18). This is being under the breaking, chastising hand of God. *"You have disciplined me,"* he says, *"I was disciplined, like an untrained calf."* This is why someone said, *"I am restless in my complaint and I moan."* Why? *"My heart is in anguish within me"* (Psalm 55:2-4).

This is grieving and lamenting to yourself in secret and closed places. You know, it is common for those people who are distressed with anguish, though all alone, to cry out to themselves about their pains, saying, "Oh, my leg! Oh, my arm! Oh, my stomach!" Or, as the son of the Shunammite, *"Oh, my head, my head!"* (2 Kings 4:19). The groans, the sighs, the cries that the brokenhearted have, when by themselves, or alone! "Oh," they say, "My sins! My sins! My soul! My soul! How I am burdened with guilt! How am I surrounded with fear! Oh, this hard, this desperate, this unbelieving heart! Oh, how sin corrupts my will, my mind, my conscience!" I am *"afflicted and close to death"* (Psalm 88:15).

If you listened at the door of his room and heard Ephraim when he was busy lamenting, it would make you stand amazed to hear him grieve about that sin in him that you take delight in. You would also hear him lamenting about misspending his time, while you spend yours pursuing your filthy lusts. You would hear him being offended with his heart, because it will not comply with God's holy will, while you are afraid of his Word and ways, and never think yourselves better than when farthest from God. The passions and lusts of the brokenhearted often make them get into a corner and lament their state.

As they cry out in grief to themselves, so they cry of and against themselves to others. *"Look and see if there is any sorrow like my sorrow"* (Lam. 1:12). What bitter cries and complaints the brokenhearted have and make to one another! They imagine that their own wounds are the deepest, and their own sores are the worst and hardest to be cured. If our iniquities are upon us, and we pine away in them, how can we then live? (Eze. 33:10).

I once asked a woman how she was doing and she said, "Very badly." I asked her if she was sick, but she answered, "No." This woman had her heart broken, she wanted Jesus, and was concerned for her soul. There are only a few people who count Jesus better than the world, their pride, and pleasures. Few people cry out like this; few are so in love with their own eternal salvation that they are willing to part with all their lusts and vanities for Jesus.

As people with broken hearts lament to one and another, so they cry to God. *"O Lord, God of my salvation, I cry out day and night before you."* This was when his soul was full of trouble, and his life drew near to the grave (Psalm 88:1). Or, as it says in another place, out of the deep, *"out of the depths I cry to you, O Lord!"* (Psalm 130:1; Jonah 2:2). These words express what a painful condition they were in when they cried.

Where does a child go when it is hurt but to its father or mother? Where does it lay its head, but in their laps? Into whose chest does it pour out its complaint, because there is pity and relief there? And so, it is the same with those whose hearts are broken. It is natural for them—they must cry; they cannot but cry to Him. *"Heal me, O Lord,"* said David, *"for my bones are troubled. My soul also is greatly troubled"* (Psalm 6:1-3). He who cannot cry feels no pain, sees no need, fears no danger, or else is dead.

Daily Reflection

When we talk about crying, we often always refer to pain. Bunyan uses this to paint a picture of how we should come to God in prayer and cry out to Him—not just in words and the volume of our prayer, but in the brokenness of our hearts. The word 'cry' is used so often in the Bible that you would think it was common for people to pray this way. It is not very common in prayers today, though, and we should strive to become people who cry out more often.

1. What does it mean to be in anguish in your heart?
2. Do you find it easy to pray this way—passionately? Why or why not?
3. Look at the book of Lamentations and read a few of the verses. Why do you think they prayed like this?
4. Psalm 130:1 talks about crying out of the depths. What does this mean, and why is it so important?
5. Why does God hear these prayers?

26

PERSEVERING IN PRAYER

"Praying at all times in the Spirit, with all prayer and supplication. To that end, keep alert with all perseverance, making supplication for all the saints"
—Ephesians 6:18

We must not be put off or tempted from our prayers.

It is good to be able to discern between good and evil and see the misery of man or the mercy of God. The pressure on a person's spirit provokes them to groan out their request to the Lord. When David felt the sorrows of hell surrounding him, he did not need a pastor to teach him to say, *"O Lord, I pray, deliver my soul!"* (Psalm 116:4). He did not need to look in a book to teach him a format to pour out his heart before God. It is the nature of the heart of people in pain and agony to vent their feelings in groans. It was the same with David in Psalm 38:1-12. And it is the same with those filled with the grace of God.

We must not be ignorant of how many tricks and temptations the devil has to make someone who is truly willing to have Jesus feel tired of seeking the face of God and think that He will not have mercy on them. Satan says, "You can pray, but you will not succeed. You can see your heart is hard, cold, and dull. You do not pray with the Spirit, you do not pray sincerely, your thoughts are running after other things—you are pretending to pray to God. Go away, hypocrite, go no further, it is all in vain to keep trying any longer!"

If we are not wise to what the devil is doing, we might cry out, *"The Lord has forsaken me; my Lord has forgotten me"* (Isa. 49:14). But someone with spiritual understanding will say, "Well, I will seek the Lord, and wait; I will not stop, even if the Lord keeps silent, and does not speak one word of comfort" (Isa. 40:27). He loved Jacob dearly, and yet he made him wrestle before he had the blessing (Gen. 32:25-27). What looks like a delay in God is not a sign of His displeasure; He might hide His face from His people (Isa. 8:17). He loves to keep his people praying, and to find them always knocking at the gate of heaven.

The soul will say, "Maybe the Lord is testing me, or He loves to hear me groan because of the condition I am in before Him." The woman of Canaan would not take Jesus' denials for real ones; she knew the Lord was gracious, and that the

Lord will avenge His people, even though he puts up with them for a long time (Luke 18:1-6). The Lord has waited longer on me than I have waited on Him. It was like this with David, *"I waited patiently for the Lord,"* he said. That means it was long before the Lord answered me, even though he eventually *"inclined"* his ear *"to me and heard my cry"* (Psalm 40:1).

The best solution for when this happens is to have a good spiritual understanding and to be well-informed and enlightened. It is unfortunate how many people there are that truly fear the Lord, but since they are not well informed in their understanding, are often quick to give up everything because of a trick and temptation of Satan! May the Lord help them to pray with the Spirit, and with discernment.

Daily Reflection

Perseverance is so often spoken about in prayer, because it is something we so easily give up when it becomes too tough, or when we feel we have not been heard for a long time. The Bible is full of the word 'wait,' which is one of the hardest things we can do. But God loves those who persevere and push through, and the rewards are often far greater once we have done so. Effective prayer is that which perseveres.

1. Why do you think it is easy for Satan to persuade us to give up?
2. What are some of the reasons that God causes us to wait or to have to persevere in prayer?
3. Do you think Jesus was exceptionally harsh on the Canaanite woman in Luke 18? Why do you think He

spoke to her as he did?
4. Do you find it difficult to keep going in prayer? Why?
5. What help does God give us when we need to persevere?

27

JESUS PRAYS FOR US

"I am praying for them. I am not praying for the world but for those whom you have given me, for they are yours"
—John 17:9

Jesus prays for all the chosen people, that they may be brought home to God, and into the unity of the faith. This is clear when he said, *"I do not ask for these only;"*—only those that are born again—*"but also for those who will believe in me through their word"*; for all those that will, that are chosen to believe; or *"for those whom you have given me"* (John 17:9, 20). And the reason is that He has paid a ransom for them.

So, when Jesus intercedes for the ungodly, and all the unconverted chosen, He petitions for His own, His purchased ones, those for whom He died, that they might be saved by His blood.

When any of these come to God, he still prays for them, that the sins that they might commit in weakness, after being born again, will also be forgiven. This is shown by the intercession of the high priest under the law, which was to remove the iniquities of the holy things of the children of Israel by his atonement for them that sinned. *"And the priest shall make atonement for him for the sin that he has committed, and he shall be forgiven"* (Lev. 5:10). This is also shown when Jesus intercedes, saying, *"I do not ask that you take them out of the world, but that you keep them from the evil one"* (John 17:15).

That Jesus prayed that those who are born again should be kept from all kinds of sin, must not be supposed, for then we make His intercession, at least in some things, invalid, and to contradict Himself; because he says, *"I knew that you always hear me"* (John 11:42). But the meaning is, I pray that You would keep them from soul-damning delusions that are unavoidable; also that You would keep them from the soul-destroying evil of every sin. He does this by His continual forgiving grace.

In his intercession, He prays also that those characteristics that we receive when we are born again will be given and maintained. This is clear as he says, *"Simon, Simon, behold, Satan demanded to have you, that he might sift you like wheat, but I have prayed for you that your faith may not fail"* (Luke 22:31-32). Some might say He is praying here for the support and supply of faith, but did He pray for the maintaining and supply of all our gifts? Yes, He prayed for the preservation of our faith, He prayed for the preservation of all our gifts because faith is the root gift, the gift that has all the others in it, and from which all others flow. It is the gift that gives life to all our other gifts.

So, if faith is preserved, then all the gifts continue and live—they function according to the present state, health, and degree of faith. So, Jesus prayed for the preservation of every gift when he prayed for the preservation of faith. That verse also has the same meaning as the one where he says, *"Keep them in your name, which you have given me"* (John 17:11). Keep them in Your fear, in the faith, in the true belief, in the way of life by Your grace, by Your power, by Your wisdom.

Daily Reflection

One of the most poignant moments in Jesus' last hours, before he was crucified, is when he prayed for the disciples. There is a depth and sincerity we can learn from in the manner he goes about it. But it is also revealing in what He prays for, to see what is important to our Lord that He should ask the Father for these things. And then, to see what should be important in our prayers as a response to that.

1. Do you think it is strange that Jesus prayed when He was and is God?
2. Why does Jesus make a distinction between the ones given to Him and the rest of the world?
3. What are the things Jesus prays for His people?

4. How does this compare with the way Paul prayed for the church in Phil:3-10?
5. Do you ever pray for others in the same fashion as our Lord prayed?

28

JESUS PRAYS FOR US (CONTINUED)

"I am praying for them. I am not praying for the world but for those whom you have given me, for they are yours"
—John 17:9

Jesus in his intercession prays that we will be preserved, and brought safe into His heavenly kingdom.

1. He prays that we will come to glory because we are His: *"Yours they were, and you gave them to me"* (John 17:6). Father, I will have them, for they are mine: *"Yours they were, and you gave them to me."* What is mine, my wife, my child, or my joy, that I may have it with me. So, He pleads or cries in his intercession, that we might be preserved to glory. They are mine, *"and you gave them to me."*

2. He also pleads that He had given—given already in the promise—glory to them, and therefore they must not go without it. *"The glory that you have given me I have given to them"* (John 17:22). Righteous people, when they give a good thing by a promise, they design the performance of that promise. More than design it, they purpose and they determine it. What incredible reassurance flows into the Christian's soul from communion with God. The wisdom of the promise lets us cast our care on our heavenly Father because all things were made by Him. He is always living to intercede for us. As the prophet also said about God in another case, *"Has he said, and will he not do it? Or has he spoken, and will he not fulfill it?"* (Num. 23:19).

3. He pleads in His interceding that they might have glory; it is His own decision to have it like that. *"Father, I desire that they also, whom you have given me, may be with me where I am"* (John 17:24). It must be so. It shall be so. I will have it so. Our Father will let Jesus have his mind and will in this since He is also as willing to have it. *"Fear not, little flock, for it is your Father's good pleasure to give you the kingdom"* (Luke 12:32). The resolution of our Intercessor is that we be preserved to glory, and this resolution he pleads in his intercession.

4. Lastly, in His intercession, He urges a reason why He will have this: *"to see my glory that you have given me because you loved me before the foundation of the world"* (John 17:24). And this is a reason for the purpose; it is as if He had said, "Father, they have continued

with Me in my temptations; they have seen Me in all my disadvantages; they have seen Me in my poor, low condition; they have seen what scorn, mocking, and disgrace I have suffered for Your sake in the world; and now I want them to also be where they will see Me in my glory. I have told them that I am Your Son, and they have believed that; I have told them that You love Me, and they have believed that; I have also told them that You would take Me again to glory, and they have believed that; but they have not seen My glory. Besides, Father, these are the ones that love Me, and it will be their joy if they can see Me in glory; it will be as heaven to their hearts to see their Savior in glory. So, I want those that *"you have given me, may be with me where I am, to see my glory."*

This is why Jesus our Lord intercedes to have His people with Him in glory.

Daily Reflection

Continuing from the previous chapter, we find Jesus goes into significant depth about the things He asks God for. Many times we want to model our prayers on a format like the Lord's Prayer, but this is merely a template. Here, we have a real-life example in the form of Jesus praying for the disciples and all those chosen, like us. To see what is important to Him and how he approached the Father should be enough of a format to mold our own prayers to.

1. What is meant by glory in this prayer of Jesus?

2. Why is it important to Jesus that we come to glory?
3. What is the promise of glory that we have already been given?
4. Does the knowledge of the glory and its promise to us change our prayers in any way?

29

THOSE WHO DO NOT PRAY

"I was ready to be sought by those who did not ask for me;
I was ready to be found by those who did not seek me.
I said, 'Here I am, here I am,' to a nation
that was not called by my name"
—Isaiah 65:1

Unfortunately, there are people who never pray at all. *"I will pray,"* (1 Cor. 14:15) said the apostle, and so those who are Christians agree and say the same thing in their hearts. You cannot be a Christian then if you are not a praying person. The promise is that every person that is righteous will pray (Psalm 32:6). If you do not pray, you are a wicked wretch.

Jacob got the name of Israel by wrestling with God (Gen. 32), and all his children and descendants bear the same name (Gal. 6:16). But those people who forget prayer, that do not call on the name of the Lord or have formal and dead prayers fall under these words: *"Pour out your wrath on the nations that know you not, and on the peoples that call not on your name"* (Jer. 10:25).

How do you like this, you who are so far from pouring out your heart before God, going to bed like a dog, rising like a lazy, selfish animal, and forgetting to call on God? What will you do when you are judged in hell because you could not find it in your heart to ask for heaven? Who will grieve for the person who did not see that mercy is worth asking for? I tell you, the ravens, the dogs, and other animals will rise up in judgment against you, because they will make a noise or show that they need food or water when they want it, but you do not have the heart to ask for heaven, even though you could perish in hell forever if you do not get heaven.

It is unbelievable to see how some people quickly forget. Those who have prayed, cried, groaned, and sighed for eternal life; those who thought no pain was too much, no way was too far, no hazard too great to run for eternal life; those who were captivated with the Word, and with the comforts and joy it brought. But now, it is as if they never were those people. The godliness they have left behind has changed their heart, mind, and ways.

It is also a warning to those who call themselves Christians either in public or private worship of God. Those who profess to be worshippers of Him must realize that the duties, like prayer, as well as the name of God, are holy, and *"among those who are near me I will be sanctified"* (Lev. 10:3). So, the person who approaches the presence of Jesus in prayer, or any other form of devotion and worship, must be careful of the *"iniquity in my heart"* (Psalm. 66:18). Otherwise, the Lord will close His ears to their prayers, and will shut His eyes, and not take notice of such kind of worship or worshippers.

What we receive depends on our hearts in prayer. Beggars used to sit with bowls in their laps when called out to passersby for food or money. And if their bowls were very small, they would come away with hardly anything, even though the generosity of the giver was large. You must become like a beggar, a beggar at God's door. Make sure you get a great big bowl, for as big as your bowl is, so will your reward be. *"According to your faith be it done to you"* (Matt. 9:29).

Daily Reflection

Unfortunately, not everyone prays, and even if they do, many stop or end up deceiving themselves into thinking they are praying when they are actually dead in their words and hearts. This is not what God wants and He often warns us against turning away or giving up. Even though we might be praying now, we also need to take this warning seriously, as we could easily be tempted to give up tomorrow.

1. What do you think of the statement: "You cannot be a Christian then if you are not a praying person"?

2. Do you think Bunyan is overly harsh in his warning and rebuke in this chapter? Why?
3. What will cause God to stop His ears to our prayers?
4. The last paragraph focuses on having faith in prayer. What correlation does this have to those who pray and those who do not?
5. Read Hebrews 10:39. What does this mean concerning this chapter?

30

THE THRONE OF GRACE

"Let us then with confidence draw near to the throne of grace, that we may receive mercy and find grace to help in time of need"
—Hebrews 4:16

We can tell the throne of grace from other thrones by the glory it always has when revealed to us by God. Its glory outshines all; there is no such glory to be seen anywhere else, either in heaven or earth. But we can only see it by the sight that God gives, not by my understanding, which is natural, blind, and foolish. When I try to reach this throne of grace and perceive its glory in my own spirit and abilities, then I am blind and foolish. I see nothing, and my heart grows flat and lifeless and has no passion for what it is doing. But when the throne is properly and truly realized, it mounts up with wings like an eagle.

This throne is the seat of grace and mercy and is called the mercy seat and throne of grace. It turns everything into grace, everything into mercy. It makes everything work together for good. King Saul's sons, in 2 Samuel 21:10-14, were not buried after they were hanged until water fell on them from heaven. It is the same for us; there is nothing that can come near us until it is washed in the water that proceeds from the throne of grace. So, hardships and trials flow from grace; persecutions flow from grace; poverty, sickness, and even death are made ours by the grace of God through Christ (Psalm 119:67-71; 1 Cor. 3:22; Rev. 3:19; Heb. 12:5-7). All things that happen to us are turned into grace for Jesus' sake.

The philosopher's stone was a myth about a stone that was believed to be able to turn everything into gold. The throne can turn everything into grace, and make all things work together for good. The grace that reigns on the throne of grace, the river that proceeds from the throne of God turns majesty, authority, glory, wisdom, faithfulness, justice, and everything into grace. John had the honor to see it, and to see the streams flowing from it. *"Then the angel showed me the river of the water of life, bright as crystal, flowing from the throne of God"* (Rev. 22:1).

During the reign of the antichrist, no one will see this throne, nor the river that comes from it. God will conceal it, and bring a cloud over it; but we will still have the preserving, saving benefits of it, even on the darkest day. And since we cannot see much, we must believe it even more; and by believing, give glory to God. We must strive to have clearer biblical knowledge of this throne because God's word is the magnifying glass that will let us see the glory of the Lord (2 Cor. 3:18).

"A throne stood in heaven, with one seated on the throne" (Rev. 4:2). That is, God. And this shows his rest forever, because sitting is rest, and Jesus is His rest forever.

It is grace that chooses, grace that calls. It is grace that preserves, and grace that brings us to glory; grace is like a river of water of life that flows from this *"throne of grace."* So, we must cry, *"Grace, grace to it!"* (Zech. 4:7).

What a throne we are invited to come to. It is a throne of grace that the God of all grace sits on. It is a throne of grace before which Jesus continually ministers for us. It is a throne of grace sprinkled with the blood, where the Lamb has been slain. It is a throne with a rainbow around it, which is the sign of the everlasting covenant, and out of which flows a pure river of water of life, clear as crystal.

Look for these signs of the throne of grace, everyone who comes to it, and do not rest until you know that you have come to it. It is there to be seen if you have eyes to see it. The sight of it is wonderful and has a tendency to revive and renew the soul.

Daily Reflection

The throne of grace is one of Bunyan's favorite topics and he discusses it a few times in his different writings. As the focal point of us coming to God in the holiest place, where He sits and hears us, it is important to understand what this throne actually is. It will help us to see in the spirit the throne room that we approach in our times of need and thanksgiving.

1. Why is it impossible to reach this throne by our own abilities?
2. What do you think about what Bunyan says here: "Hardships and trials flow from grace; persecutions flow from grace; poverty, sickness, and even death is made ours by the grace of God through Christ"?
3. What is grace? Read Ephesians 2:8-9.
4. What is the difference between the throne of grace and the judgment seat?
5. How does this throne of grace relate to prayer?

31

COMING BOLDLY TO THE THRONE

"Let us then with confidence draw near to the throne of grace, that we may receive mercy and find grace to help in time of need"
—Hebrews 4:16

We are told to come boldly. It is done through the blood of Jesus and through the sanctifying of the Spirit which is received by faith. There is no boldness, godly boldness, but by blood. The further we are from the blood, the further we are from being bold with God, at the throne of grace; for it is the blood that makes the atonement, and that gives boldness to the soul (Lev. 17:11; Heb. 10:19).

It is the blood, the power of it by faith that drives away guilt and fear and brings boldness. If we want to be bold with God at the throne of grace, we must first be acquainted with the blood of Jesus—it was shed and has made peace with God. We must be able, by faith, to be counted as those who share in this reconciliation before we can come boldly to the throne of grace.

"Let us draw near with a true heart in full assurance of faith" (Heb. 10:22). It is our privilege, duty, and glory to approach the throne of grace as princes.

But what about Job? He said, *"Oh, that I knew where I might find him, that I might come even to his seat! I would lay my case before him and fill my mouth with arguments. I would know what he would answer me and understand what he would say to me. Would he contend with me in the greatness of his power? No; he would pay attention to me. There an upright man could argue with him, and I would be acquitted forever by my judge"* (Job 23:3-7).

Sometimes God tests us. *"He covers the face of the full moon and spreads over it his cloud"* (Job 26:9). And this seems to be Job's case here, which made him confess he was at a loss, and he cried out, "Oh, that I knew where I might find him!" God does this to prove our honesty and perseverance because the hypocrite will not always pray. Will he always call on God? No, especially when God tests them, brings hardships, and makes praying hard work for them (Job 36:13).

But the difficulty in finding God's presence and His throne does not always lie in the weakness of faith. Strong faith was needed even though it was hard to keep standing. God hid the face of his throne and spread a cloud over it; not to weaken Job's faith, but to test his strength, and to show us how courageous he was. Faith, if it is strong, will keep us strong in the dark. We will not be discouraged in trials— *"Though he slay me, I will hope in him"* (Job 13:15).

Daily Reflection

If you have worked through these daily reflections and been open and honest, then with the Holy Spirit's help, He will teach and show you many things, and your prayer life will be enriched as you grow in these areas. To admit our weaknesses and see how the Lord wants to guide and lead us into so much more, is to open the way for growth and maturity.

1. What does it mean to come 'boldly'? Is it arrogance and confidence?
2. Why do we sometimes find it difficult to draw near to the throne of grace, without feeling bold?
3. Do you sometimes feel like Job when he could not find the throne and did not know where to go?
4. Why does God test us like this? What should our response be in these times?

IF YOU ENJOYED this 31-day prayer guide and you would like to do more, you can look out for others in the series from different classic Christian writers:

- E.M. Bounds Prayer: *31 Life-Changing Insights From E.M. Bounds on How to Pray With Daily Reflections*

- J.C. Ryle on Prayer: *31 Insights for Understanding the Purpose and Power of Prayer*
- C.H. Spurgeon on Prayer: *31 Effective Insights on How to Pray With Daily Reflections*

ABOUT JOHN BUNYAN

John Bunyan was born in 1628 to Thomas Bunyan and Margaret Bentley in Bedfordshire, England. As ordinary villagers, they did not have the luxury of being able to afford a decent education, and John was most likely taught at his home along with other boys of the same poor class. He may have attended a local school at some point, but somewhere along the way, he developed a high degree of literacy.

He soon took on the job of tinker, something his father may have also practiced. This would involve a fair amount of traveling to fix and mend pots, pans, and any other metal utensils. After his mother and sister died in 1644, at the age of 16, John left to join the Parliamentary army working at the Newport Pagnell garrison.

As the English Civil War drew to a close in 1647, John returned to the trade of tinker. He had no real sense of Christianity and spent his days doing what other carefree young men did during those times. Sport, dancing, and enjoying his free moments were all that mattered. Being quick with his tongue, he was known by his friends as "the ungodliest fellow for swearing they ever heard."

But Bunyan was haunted by dreams and visions. He claimed to have heard a voice that challenged him to live in sin and go to hell or give up that life and enter heaven. This would be the beginning of his struggle with guilt and trying to understand damnation and salvation.

At the age of 22, he married, though the couple were not well-off and remained "as poor as poor might be." During this time, he read and became convicted of giving his life up to serve Christ. Having learned under a man called John Gifford, Bunyan took over the job of preaching in 1655. In the next two years, he became a minister in St. John's Church and published his books *Some Gospel Truths* and *Vindication*.

His preaching was popular with some and gained him criticism from others. By the time Charles II became king, Bunyan's persecution truly began as the country adopted Anglicanism against all other doctrines. He was arrested on 12 November 1660 and sent to jail. When asked if he would give up his preaching, he responded by saying, "If you release me today, I will preach tomorrow."

During his imprisonment at Bedford Jail, he worked on his most famous book, an allegory of the Christian journey called *The Pilgrim's Progress*. After being in and out of jail over the next 12 years, Bunyan would continue to preach to inmates, play music on homemade instruments, and write. In a pardon from the king, secured by the Quakers, he was finally released. In 1687, King James II offered him a royal position to oversee Bedford, but he declined, preferring his simple life of preaching.

John Bunyan died on 31 August 1688 after catching a cold while out riding to a friend's house.

BIBLIOGRAPHY

Chaplin, J. (2022). *The Riches of Bunyan*. Gutenberg.org. https://www.gutenberg.org/cache/epub/5831/pg5831.txt

Crossway. (2001). *English Standard Version Bible*. Crossway Bibles.

Digital Puritan Press. (n.d.). *John Bunyan*. Digitalpuritan.net. http://digitalpuritan.net/john-bunyan/

www.ingramcontent.com/pod-product-compliance
Lightning Source LLC
LaVergne TN
LVHW020439070526
838199LV00063B/4786